MARXIST MONEY

CENTRAL BANK DIGITAL CURRENCIES AND THE THEFT OF FREEDOM

BY **MATHEW D. STAVER, ESQ.**
AND **STEPHANIE BOWEN**

Marxist Money:
Central Bank Digital Currencies and the Theft of Freedom
by Mathew D. Staver, Esq., and Stephanie Bowen

New Revolution
Creative Communication & Printing Services
NewRevolution.org

Copyright © 2024 New Revolution

Edited by Christine D. Johnson
Cover design and layout by Stuart Letizia

Printed in the United States of America

POLITICAL SCIENCE/Religion, Politics & State
ISBN: 979-8-218-98807-4

For my father, who taught me how to reason.
—S.B.

CONTENTS

Preface 1

Chapter 1: All About Control 3
   Executive Order 14067 5
   Project Hamilton 7

Chapter 2: How Money Has Changed 9
   The Federal Reserve 10
   The Gold Standard 12

Chapter 3: CBDC vs. Crypto 15
   Free Market Cryptocurrencies 17
   Cash and Control 20

Chapter 4: Digital Dollars Around the World 23
   China 23
   Europe 28

Chapter 5: The Central Bankers' Central Banks 31
   IMF 32
   Bank for International Settlements 33
   SWIFT 35
   Absolute Control Is the Endgame 39

Chapter 6: Past is Prologue 43
   Propaganda on the Rise 50
   Economic Freedom: The Basis of Liberty 51

Appendices 55
   Executive Order 14067 55
   Bitcoin White Paper 72

Endnotes 81

About 86

PREFACE

A new global push is propelling Americans closer to a Revelation 13 reality, where one is not allowed to buy or sell freely without government permission and control.

Central Bank Digital Currencies (CBDCs) are being proposed around the world in order to control the people by controlling their money. These digital programmable dollars are designed to replace cold hard cash, while giving bureaucrats complete access to, and control over, every cent people earn, spend and store.

Communist China already utilizes this technology, and the consequences have been dire. The Chinese Communist Party (CCP) uses CBDCs to prevent citizens from spending their own hard-earned money as they please. Chinese citizens are even prevented from paying for medical services and medicine when the CCP determines that person has used too many healthcare resources.

Now, at the demand of Joe Biden, the U.S. Federal Reserve has created their own Central Bank Digital Currency, and we are in a race to protect Americans and their freedom from politicians hellbent on imposing control over every life. Without hyperbole, CBDCs have the power to place people in digital prisons.

We've written this book to help inform you of the dangers ahead, and measures we can take now to protect the future. Please share this information with others, and especially your elected officials.

Freedom is precious. Once lost, it is difficult to regain.
Let's make sure we don't lose it on our watch.

Mathew D. Staver, Esq.

Founder & Chairman, Liberty Counsel
Founder & Chairman, New Revolution
Chairman, Liberty Counsel Action

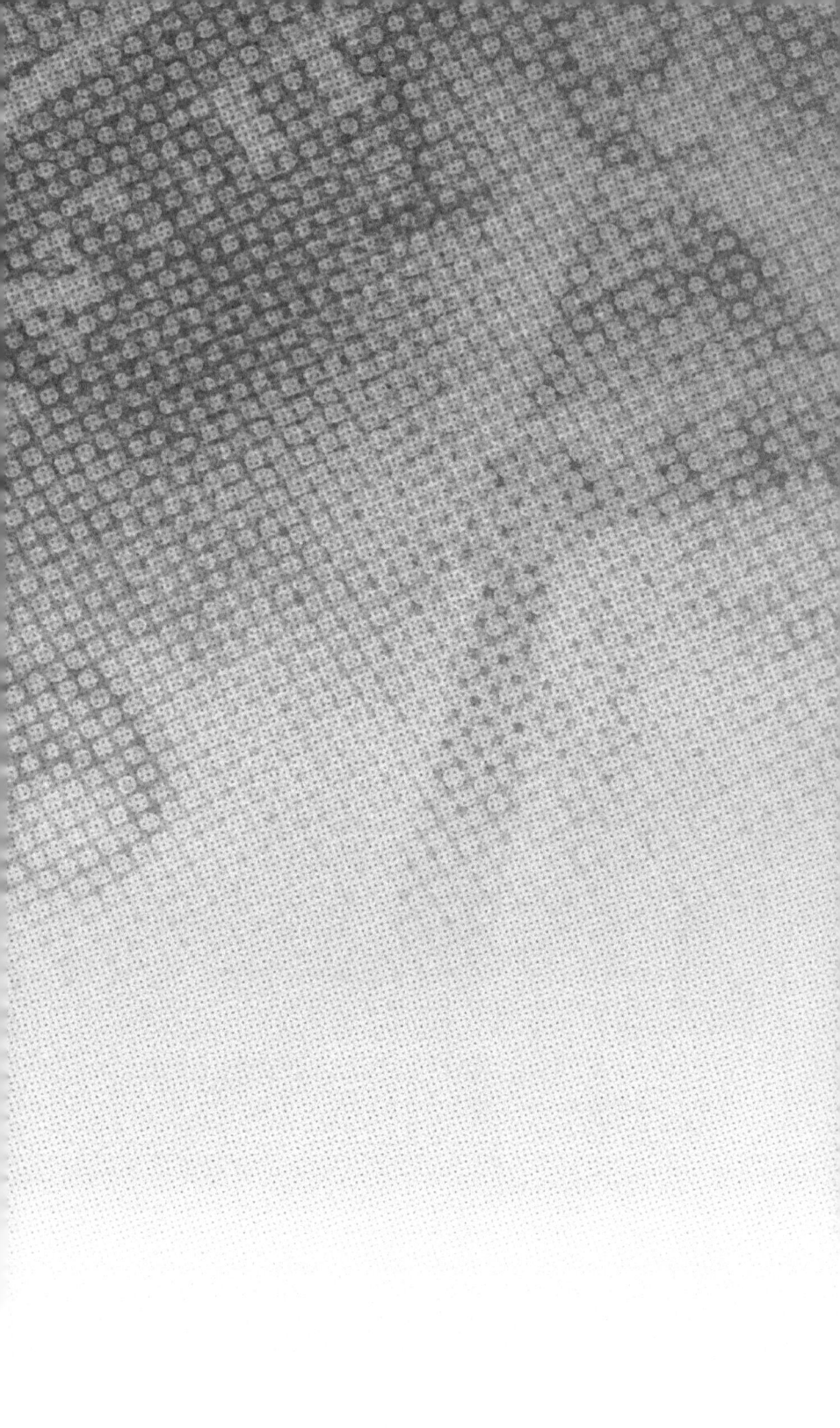

CHAPTER 1

ALL ABOUT CONTROL

In Karl Marx's quest to fundamentally control populations, he demanded "centralization of credit in the hands of the State, by means of a national bank with State capital and an exclusive monopoly."

Marx knew that to control the man, one must control the man's finances. Now globalists around the world are seeking to do just that by eliminating cash money and local bank accounts, replacing them with programmable "digital dollars," issued by government central banks directly to consumers.

Called Central Bank Digital Currencies (CBDCs), these programmable digital dollars allow the government to know everything about your spending, savings, and more. The government will be able to coerce or veto your spending. A CBDC will even allow political "equity" agendas to skim value off the top of your dollar and shift it to another person.

"The potential expansion of the money supply, and the Fed gaining new powers by stepping into the commercial banking/government transferor/collection agency role, is most concerning if not completely terrifying," says Robert Aro of economic think tank Mises Institute.[1]

Once the government is your bank, not only can they spy on your every financial transaction without a warrant or due process, but then the government can also control your money and, thereby, your actions, any time they want. So called "climate change" initiatives can be enforced with the touch of a button. "Woke" dictates like ESG (environmental, social and governance initiatives), and wealth redistribution could also be easily enforced.

With a push of a button, bureaucrats could inflate the certain peoples' CBDCs, while *deflating* the value of other people's funds—all in the name of equity, progressivism, and yes, even reparations.

And because—cash will have been eliminated, there will be no way around, or out of, the new tyrannical system.

In 2022, the Federal Reserve issued a report entitled *"Money and Payments: The U.S. Dollar in the Age of Digital Information."* [2]

In it, the Fed argues, "A widely available CBDC would serve as a close—or, in the case of an interest-bearing CBDC, near-perfect—substitute for commercial bank money."

In other words, the government wants to become your bank, eliminating commercial bank "competition" and ending the use of cold, hard cash.

According to economist Robert Murphy, "If average Americans hold bank accounts directly with the Fed, its control over their lives would be nearly absolute, particularly if cash is phased out."[3] That kind of control could be expressed in a multitude of ways, depending on who holds power in the White House, Congress, or even the United Nations.

A CBDC gives the federal government the power to prevent you from spending or saving your own money as you choose.

Communist China already employs such financial surveillance and control, and now some in the United States government are trying to seize that tyrannical power as well.

Just over one year after his presidency began, Joe Biden issued an executive order that, if fully implemented, will destroy whatever is left of American liberty and the free market system.

The Federal Reserve has already begun acting on that order, taking the initial steps to create and issue a new programmable digital dollar designed to monitor and dictate your every move.

EXECUTIVE ORDER 14067

On March 9, 2022, Joe Biden issued Executive Order 14067[4], entitled "Ensuring Responsible Development of Digital Assets."

Through this device, Biden ordered the Federal Reserve to begin "investigating" Central Bank Digital Currencies for use in America.

> *By the authority vested in me as President by the Constitution and the laws of the United States of America, it is hereby ordered as follows:*
>
> **Section 1.** *Policy. Advances in digital and distributed ledger technology for financial services have led to dramatic growth in markets for digital assets, with profound implications for the protection of consumers, investors, and businesses, including data privacy and security; financial stability and systemic risk; crime; national security; the ability to exercise human rights; financial inclusion and equity; and energy demand and climate change.*

In November 2021, non-state issued digital assets reached a combined market capitalization of $3 trillion, up from approximately $14 billion in early November 2016.

Monetary authorities globally are also exploring, and in some cases introducing, central bank digital currencies (CBDCs). While many activities involving digital assets are within the scope of existing domestic laws and regulations, an area where the United States has been a global leader, growing development and adoption of digital assets and related innovations, as well as inconsistent controls to defend against certain key risks, necessitate an evolution and alignment of the United States Government approach to digital assets.

The United States has an interest in responsible financial innovation, expanding access to safe and affordable financial services, and reducing the cost of domestic and cross-border funds transfers and payments, including through the continued modernization of public payment systems.

We must take strong steps to reduce the risks that digital assets could pose to consumers, investors, and business protections; financial stability and financial system integrity; combating and preventing crime and illicit finance; national security; the ability to exercise human rights; financial inclusion and equity; and climate change and pollution.[5]

The Federal Reserve took that executive order and ran with it, hiring software developers to create and test this new digital currency.

PROJECT HAMILTON

On December 22, 2022, the Boston Federal Reserve, in collaboration with the Massachusetts Institute of Technology (MIT), finished testing the first American prototype for a CBDC.[6] Called "Project Hamilton," the program was named for America's first treasury secretary, Alexander Hamilton.

Hamilton, a dyed-in-the-wool federalist, believed the central government should be stronger and have more power than the state governments. Though the newly minted U.S. Constitution found a balance between federal and state rights, Hamilton found a way to increase the central government's power—by controlling the money.

Hamilton was the key thought leader behind America's first central bank.[7] He understood the biblical admonition that the borrower is always slave to the lender (Proverbs 22:7). Using this to his advantage, Hamilton proposed the federal government buy up each revolutionary state's war debt.

In 1789, President George Washington appointed Hamilton as the nation's first treasury secretary. By 1791, Hamilton's scheme became reality, and **the First Bank of the United States** was born.

———

The federal government now controlled the states via their debt, and the money those states would be allowed to use. Fast-forward 230 years or so, and Hamilton's plan could hardly have worked better.

CHAPTER 2

HOW MONEY HAS CHANGED

To understand CBDCs, one must first understand the basis of U.S. monetary policy. To fully appreciate what CBDCs are and how they will be used, it's important to understand what our money is now, and what it used to be.

At the height of the British Empire, silver and gold were the primary payment method for international trade. The British Empire spanned the entire globe. To keep payments efficient, the British required their colonies to adopt a gold standard.

Prior to the U.S. Civil War, the United States also used gold and silver as official currency. However, mounting debt from the Civil War prompted a change. In 1862, Illinois businessman Edmond Dick Taylor proposed issuing paper currency backed by nothing other than the full faith and credit of the United States. Desperate for cash to pay soldiers and laborers, Congress adopted the idea, passing the Legal Tender Act on February 25, 1862.[8] The new law authorized the issuance of 150 million paper notes, called "greenbacks," the equivalent of $4.7 million in 2024 dollars.

But there was a problem with the federal government's valueless paper money—states would not accept it. California and Oregon openly defied the Legal Tender Act. Merchants in those states blacklisted people who attempted to make payments with the paper money, banks refused to accept the bills for deposits, and the states themselves refused to accept the greenbacks as tax payments.[9]

By 1873, the U.S. government's initial foray into fiat money was over. The U.S. officially adopted the gold standard.

Germany followed suit that same year. The rest of the world followed, and by the end of the 19th century, nearly all international currencies were pegged to the value of gold.[10]

After World War I, however, both the United Kingdom and Germany were heavily in debt, and did not have the gold reserves to pay their debt. So they started issuing paper fiat money, backed by nothing more than full faith and credit of those governments. In contrast, the United States remained on the gold standard.

THE FEDERAL RESERVE

The Federal Reserve, aka "the Fed," was created in 1913 to stabilize the financial sector. The Federal Reserve Act of 1913 required the Federal Reserve to have gold backing 40% of its bank certificates, which, at the time, citizens could redeem for their worth in gold coins.

The Fed went about buying up much of the world's gold supply. This included selling U.S. citizens Victory Bonds, which the government had promised would be redeemable in gold coin. The expansion of the Federal Reserve's gold supply helped set the foundation for America becoming a world superpower. By 1919, for the first time in its history, America become a net creditor country, as opposed to a net debtor on the world stage.

Great Britain did return to the gold standard, briefly, in 1925, but it was short lived. In 1931, Great Britain abandoned gold once and for all.[11] Other countries, impoverished by the war and depression, followed suit.

In his landmark book, Gold and Economic Freedom, former Chairman of the Federal Reserve Alan Greenspan noted that Great Britain's decision to abandon the gold standard caused the Great Depression.

"Great Britain fared even worse, and rather than absorb the full consequences of her previous folly, she abandoned the gold standard completely in 1931, tearing asunder what remained of the fabric of confidence and inducing a world-wide series of bank failures," Greenspan wrote in 1966.[12]

The problem of sovereign debt was not limited to Great Britain or Europe. By the late 1920s, the Federal Reserve had reached the limit of its available credit via the terms Congress had set in 1913. It simply did not hold enough gold to cover 40% of the currency it had issued.

The Fed began to claim that the gold standard limited the flexibility of the central bank's monetary policy by limiting its ability to expand the money supply, i.e., print more money.

On April 4, 1933, exactly one month and one day after becoming president of the United States, Franklin D. Roosevelt issued Executive Order 6102.[13] That order shook the very foundations of American liberty. Roosevelt claimed that Americans dutifully saving money were "hoarders," implying that these wise and frugal folks were responsible for the Great Depression. Within a year of Roosevelt's seizure of American citizens' gold, all Federal Reserve-affiliated banks also were required to turn their gold over to the U.S. Treasury.

> FDR's order demanded that **every single American** turn over whatever gold coins, bars, or gold certificates they had to the U.S. government within just 30 days.
>
> Failure to obey would result in up to
> **10 years in prison and fines of up to $10,000**
> ($241,953 in 2024 dollars).[14]

Gold stores were exchanged for pieces of government printed paper, which Roosevelt had arbitrarily devalued by 40%. That devaluation meant that for every dollar's worth of gold a citizen or bank turned over, the U.S. government gave that person a piece of paper worth just 60 cents. The federal government's scheme, shorting people 40% of what they were promised, is perhaps the ultimate expression of what the Bible calls "unjust weights and measures."

The gold seizure enabled the Federal to expand the monetary supply, albeit on the backs of the Americans they had shorted. Many more dollars floated around, but they were worth *less*.

The process particularly rankled Americans who had purchased government Liberty Bonds to help fund World War I war efforts. Though the bond contract required the bondholder to be repaid in gold, the government instead repaid them in devalued paper, i.e., fiat money.

Several Americans sued the government for this outrageous breach of contract and violation of liberty. Sadly, in *Perry v. United States*, the Supreme Court of that time upheld the seizures as constitutional.[15]

It would remain illegal to own any but the smallest amounts of gold, other than jewelry and dental devices, until 1974 when President Gerald Ford signed into law legislation to "permit United States citizens to purchase, hold, sell, or otherwise deal with gold in the United States or abroad."[16]

Though Roosevelt took money out of citizens' hands, gold still remained the standard upon which the American government paid other countries, albeit at Roosevelt's reduced valuation.

THE GOLD STANDARD

In July 1944, delegates from 44 countries met in Bretton Woods, New Hampshire, for the United Nations Monetary and Financial Conference.[17] The summit was largely the dream child of British economist John Maynard Keynes and the U.S. Treasury Department's chief international economist Harry Dexter White.[18]

Keynes wanted to establish a global central bank and a singular international currency. White, on the other hand, wanted the U.S. dollar to play a stronger role in international finance. They both got what they wanted. Over three weeks, the delegates developed an agreement for foreign exchange and took measures to prevent countries from engaging in unfair competition by devaluing their currencies.

This was achieved by requiring all member currencies to peg their value to the U.S. dollar, which, in turn, would be pegged to the price of gold. They also created the International Monetary Fund (IMF) and the World Bank.

The Bretton Woods Agreement would remain in place until 1971, when President Richard Nixon removed America from the gold standard altogether. Nixon declared that payments to foreign countries would no longer be made in gold or certificates redeemable in gold. Foreign countries were forced to accept paper fiat dollars, backed by nothing other than the full faith and credit of the U.S. government.

To this day, U.S. money remains "fiat" money, meaning that it is backed by nothing other than the full faith and credit of the U.S. government.

> As of this writing, the U.S. government is
> **$34,874,036,000,000**
> —that's **$34 trillion**—in debt.[19]

Furthermore, America's debt to GDP (Gross Domestic Product) ratio is 89.4%. That means the U.S. government owes 89 cents of every dollar produced in the entire country to debt. Certainly, some of that debt is to America's own people, via Treasury Notes and the like. However, 86.51% of that debt is owed to **foreign** creditors, like the government of China.[20]

The debt load becomes staggering when one includes our government's "unfunded liabilities." Unfunded liabilities include Social Security, Medicare parts A, B, and D, along with federal employee and military veteran pensions and benefits.

When all of that debt is compiled, the total U.S. debt is over $219 trillion.

To put that number into perspective, that's *219 thousand billion*, and it is more than the entire net worth of every single man, woman, child, and business in America *combined*. As of August 2024, the total net worth of every single man, woman, child, small business, and large American corporation is only $214 trillion—5 trillion less than all the government's debt. And that debt is increasing by $1 trillion every 100 days.[21]

With a debt load like that, it's hard to argue that America is a creditworthy country. The reality is the U.S. dollar has been worthless since it came off the gold standard, and therefore, is really only backed by the power and might of the U.S. military.

To be fair, no country uses the gold standard anymore, having long traded their gold stores to escape debt incurred by profligate government spending. So now virtually all currencies are fiat currencies. Instead of having a fixed standard (gold) to dictate the value of a currency, the value of money is dictated by the whims of governments that manipulate its value to enforce domestic and global policies via central banks.

One notable outlier is the country of El Salvador, which has declared Bitcoin to be legal tender and an official currency.[22]

CHAPTER 3

CBDC VS. CRYPTO

There are two types of CBDC—wholesale and retail.

Biden's executive order did not distinguish between the two, but there are important differences.

Wholesale CBDC is intended to be used between countries and for international and business-to-business transactions. Today, if you were to buy a product from a merchant in a foreign country, your payment would have to go through multiple hands, each adding fees, before the payment arrives at the merchant's business.

If the merchant does not accept U.S. credit cards, the payment first goes through your bank, then to the central bank (in America, the Federal Reserve), which then sends the payment through an international central bank clearing system before those funds are sent to the receiving business' bank, then finally to the merchant. That process generally takes 5-7 business days, and each central bank or clearing system charges a hefty fee along the way for their rather laggard service.

This is true for multimillion-dollar business-to-business transactions, as well as smaller consumer-to-business purchases. So, whether you are a U.S.- based individual trying to buy a $100 worth of sunscreen or a wholesaler trying to buy $1,000,000 worth of sunscreen from a Croatia-based business, that payment goes through the central banks. Even Visa credit card payments run through the international central bank clearinghouse, known as SWIFT.[23]

Proponents claim that a CBDC is necessary to make international transactions faster and more secure. However, as we will see later in this chapter, those claims are demonstrably false.

Retail CBDC, on the other hand, is intended to be issued to individuals, replacing cold, hard cash with a digital programmable dollar. There are several deeply concerning elements to this plan. While many CBDC proponents have claimed that the U.S. government only wants to use digital currency for international wholesale transactions, MIT's analysis of the project shows otherwise.

In January 2023, MIT's Digital Currency Initiative released its report on their collaboration with the *Federal Reserve Bank of Boston* on Project Hamilton.[24]

> **The Executive Summary of that report states:**
>
> "Our primary goal was to design a core transaction processor that meets the robust speed, throughput, and fault tolerance requirements of a large *retail payment system*" (emphasis added).

In fact, as noted in the MIT report, the primary focus on testing the CBDC was to see if it could handle massive numbers of transactions each second. In other words, whether the government's digital money could operate as fast and as well as personal retail credit and debit cards or cryptocurrency transactions.

The MIT report notes several serious issues with the test. One alarming issue was the failure to control accidental "double spends," i.e., charging twice for the same purchase. However, despite MIT citing problems with the CBDC, the Boston Federal Reserve declared the project to be a success.

FREE MARKET CRYPTOCURRENCIES

"It is important to understand that the digital dollar would *not* be similar to cryptocurrencies like bitcoin," writes Justin Haskins, director of the Socialism Research Center at The Heartland Institute. *"Cryptocurrencies operate on blockchain technology, which is decentralized by design. No group or individual can truly control cryptocurrencies once they are launched,"* Haskins adds.[25]

Central Bank Digital Currencies use much of the same technology as cryptocurrencies, with one highly significant difference—they insert a government or central bank in the middle of every transaction, which creates fees and allows the go-between full access and control over every financial transaction, no matter how small.

According to Brookings Institute, cryptocurrencies are "a form of payment that can circulate without the need for a central monetary authority such as a government or bank." These technologies "enable people to buy, sell or trade" in total privacy with no government intermediary to snoop, stop, or control the transaction.[26]

Perhaps the best example of a free-market cryptocurrency is Bitcoin.

> **Bitcoin** was invented in 2008 by **Satoshi Nakamoto**[27] to create a true free market currency that cannot be controlled by governments or central banks.

Bitcoin was designed to replace the world money supply, which, at the time of Bitcoin development, was $21 trillion. Each Bitcoin was designed to be worth $100,000,000 when the cryptocurrency reaches full adoption. Each Bitcoin is broken down into smaller increments, known as "Satoshis." There are a fixed number of Bitcoins, 21 million, meaning no one will ever be able devalue the existing Bitcoins by making more of them.

Contrast that with America's Federal Reserve, which uses programs like "quantitative easing" (i.e., printing more money) to increase the monetary supply, which, in turn, lowers the value of every dollar with each new fiat dollar printed.

Bitcoin was reportedly created as a stopgap against Communist China's currency manipulation and control measures, as well as central bank control over world economics, by putting the control of money into the user's hands without government or central bank interference changing the value of that money.

Cryptocurrencies like Bitcoin are permissionless.

Anyone can use cryptocurrency without government permission and can use those funds however they want—without government oversight or control. That decentralization means cryptocurrencies give users "full ownership and control" of their own money.[28]

Cryptocurrencies are decentralized.

There is no central authority or government controlling the currency. Cryptocurrencies cannot be seized, manipulated, or frozen by central bank government authorities.

"Because no one can increase the supply of Bitcoin beyond its predetermined mining schedule, no one can arbitrarily erode its value like the U.S. government has done with the dollar through money-printing," says economist Brad Polumbo.[29]

But where cryptocurrencies are designed to be private and secure, CBDCs are designed for government financial surveillance and control.

Bitcoin's rising popularity "left many government bureaucrats feeling left out," Polumbo says. So those bureaucrats decided to produce their own digital currency—one designed to counteract and eliminate all the privacies and securities Bitcoin had created.

> Blockchain security specialist Reuben Jackson agrees.
>
> **"Financial regulators are already worried about losing control over the money supply given the rising adoption of Bitcoin and other cryptocurrencies."**
>
> *(emphasis added)*

In other words, governments and central banks are exasperated by the financial privacy cryptocurrencies provide.

"The ugly aspect of CBDCs is that they centralize money even more and preserve the oligopoly power of financial institutions," Jackson said.

"Unlike cryptocurrencies that aim to democratize and decentralize finance, CBDCs grant near-complete control to central banks."

"Central banks can conceivably use their new digital toolkits to monitor, record, analyze and tax every transaction," says Jackson, who added that CBDCs "would also enhance control over an ordinary citizen's level of access to a financial system, especially if a citizen is engaging in behavior that central banks may deem threatening, for whatever reason."[30]

> **In contrast to cryptocurrencies, CBDCs are both permission-based and centralized.**

Because CBDCs are both permission-based and run by central banks, they give a government (and their globalist central banker pals) the ability to control the money supply with the press of a button, inflating or deflating the value of those digital "dollars"—and entire economies—at their whim.

CBDCs are being created by the central bank "middlemen," continuing the central bankers' scheme of controlling and profiting off the transfer of money around the world. Because the digital currencies are not fixed to a final total number, like Bitcoin and other cryptocurrencies, the programmable nature of the CBDCs means governments are able to manipulate their monetary values even more easily—literally at a touch of a button, no printing or coin minting necessary.

The decline of the U.S. dollar since leaving the gold standard illustrates central bank currency manipulation all too well. Since abandoning the gold standard in 1971, the dollar has lost 98% of its value. What cost just 2 cents in 1971 now costs 1 dollar.[31]

The change in value is not a result of corporations increasing prices, but rather a reflection of the Federal Reserve imposing unjust weights and measures, printing money out of thin air, thereby reducing the value of every dollar bill it prints.

CASH AND CONTROL

CBDCs are anything but private or anonymous. Instead, CBDCs make the federal government your bank. And as your banker, the government does not need a warrant to snoop on the details of your account—every single transaction is right in front of them.

CBDCs also eliminate cash and the privacy it offers. At present, there is a retail commercial bank between user funds and the Federal Reserve. However, a retail CBDC would be a direct liability of the Federal Reserve, meaning that the Fed will issue those funds directly to the consumer, eliminating the need for a retail bank.

In other words, the government becomes your direct bank. Instead of storing cash in a private bank, the central bank gives the user a digital wallet—owned and operated by the central bank—for the storage and use of digital funds.

> **"The ultimate goal,"**
> says Dr. Joseph Mercola,
> **"is total control over every human body and mind."**
>
> ———•◆•———
>
> He writes:
> **"In the end, everything will be connected to a single implantable device** that will hold your digital identity, health data and programmable CBDCs.

"Your digital identity, in turn, will include **everything** that can be known about you through surveillance via implanted biosensors, your computer, smartphone, GPS, social media, online searches, purchases and spending habits.

Algorithms will then decide **what you can and cannot do** based on who you are."[32] *(emphasis added)*

If a CBDC replaces cold hard cash, the government will become your bank, able to see and control every transaction you make, including whether and how you are allowed to use your funds.

In fact, in some areas around the world, this is already being done.

CHAPTER 4

DIGITAL DOLLARS AROUND THE WORLD

Multiple nations around the world are developing their own CBDCs. As government control is at the heart of centralizing the use of currency around the world, it should come as no surprise that the government of the second largest country in the world is already using it to their advantage.

CHINA

The People's Republic of China began developing its CBDC, known as the "digital yuan" or digital renminbi (RMB), in 2014, alongside the CCP's social credit system. According to a Chinese Communist Party (CCP) document published at the time, the social credit system seeks to reinforce the idea that "keeping trust is glorious and breaking trust is disgraceful."[33] China's CBDC is used to enforce the CCP's social behavior demands, enslaving the people to the party's whims.

> "The eventual 'end-state' of the system,"
> *according to Horizons, a global workforce payment program,*
> "is a unified record for people, businesses, and the government, which can be monitored in real-time."[34]

Emily Jin of the Center for a New American Security says, "Chinese policymakers are trying to not just create a technical infrastructure, but an institutional environment that makes this kind of currency that has social control implications more acceptable in the long run."[35]

> *The CCP went to great lengths to incentivize citizens to adopt the CBDC, including depositing "free digital money" into citizen accounts and giving away digital money for CCP-approved behavior, such as "performing heroic deeds" or praising communism online.*
>
> *CCP-owned banks offered "free" CBDC money to be deposited in the accounts of newlyweds who chose to marry at official offices.*

As the number of people who used the CBDC grew, so did CCP control over the users. Yaya J. Fanusie, also with the Center for a New American Security, notes that the CCP has now developed applications that determine and enforce the CCP's will on citizen budgets, including earmarking funds for health care or travel.[36] Once the CCP distributes the funds, they cannot be used for any other purpose other than that assigned.

If the citizen runs out of those health care or travel funds, the citizen will be barred from receiving medical treatment or using transportation even if the individual has other non-earmarked funds available.

> But it's even worse than that, according to Jin, who says the project has political motivations.

> If the CCP doesn't like what the citizen has been buying, it will simply limit the citizen's ability to spend money or completely erase the citizen's life savings!
>
> If a Chinese citizen obeys and publicly praises the CCP, the citizen is given extra money, low interest rates, and the freedom to spend largely as they wish.

But if citizens dare question CCP policies—or are known Christians—they will face heavy restrictions on their ability to use their own money. The CCP considers Christianity to be a "cult," and therefore uses its CBDC as a means to punish Christians and discourage others from learning more about the Good News of Jesus Christ.

As a result, Chinese Christians are denied loans and consumer credit, are barred from paying for private school tuition, and can only use their own hard-earned money to buy what the CCP *allows* them to buy.

And if those Christians spread the gospel online or are known to question the CCP, their funds are simply erased, impoverishing individuals and their family members as punishment. All it takes is the push of a single button to erase the financial freedom of dissenters.

> "If somebody goes crosswise with the government, suddenly their e-wallets could disappear, or they can't even get in a taxi or go to a restaurant,"
>
> says Jeremy Mark, a senior fellow with the Atlantic Counsel, a Washington, D.C., international affairs think tank, commenting on China's financial surveillance system.[37]

In 2018 alone, 23 million Chinese citizens were prevented from using their own money to purchase plane and bus tickets because the CCP had determined they were guilty of "**poor social credit**" and "**behavior crimes**."[38]

One documented case tells the story all too well:

A Chinese citizen recently jaywalked across a metropolitan street. In real time, the man's face was immediately displayed on the billboards above to publicly shame him, and a fine was instantly assessed and payment taken from his CBDC account.[39] *There was no opportunity for appeal or due process. The man's money simply vanished from his account to pay the fine.*

Another incident happened to the son of a pastor with whom I am acquainted. Johnny* had taken what he thought was the opportunity of a lifetime—an internship with a major Chinese company.

In his free time, Johnny took what was supposed to be a three-day weekend from China to visit Malaysia. Unfortunately, he fell ill in the island nation and had to be hospitalized. Johnny dutifully alerted his Chinese boss, who then dutifully alerted the Chinese government.

The Chinese government immediately froze Johnny's entire Chinese bank account, nearly $7,000—a fortune for a 20-year-old. The CCP also tried to order the Malaysian hospital, where Johnny was being treated, to seize the young American's passport...

> *The CCP had Johnny over a barrel. Johnny was told that if he returned to China immediately, his money and social credits would be restored, but only if he did exactly as the party told him...*
>
> ---
>
> *Johnny was broke and paperless, stuck in a foreign country, and at the whim of the CCP. Thanks to friends with international connections, he was able to return to the U.S. However, he was never able to gain access to his Chinese government-controlled bank account.*

The CCP goes even further to enforce Communist Party ideals, using its CBDC to dictate citizens' spending habits, effectively "vetoing" consumer purchases with which the CCP disagrees.

For instance, if the CCP believes a citizen has used too much gasoline for the month, his or her CBDC will be rejected at the pump—even if plenty of funds are available in the citizen's account. If the CCP believes a citizen has used too many health care resources, that person will no longer be able to use their own money to pay for doctors, treatments, or medications.

> And if a person belongs to a disfavored religion, like Christianity, the funds can be erased, and the Christian is left with nothing.
>
> But, if you think only the bad guys in the CCP are using this to control their people, think again.

EUROPE

With governments around the world planning and implementing CBDCs, not one of the governments or central bankers have designed their CBDCs to pay interest, according to a 2021 Goldman Sachs report.[40]

The report also notes that these central bankers are considering *setting a penalty on holdings above a certain threshold.*

And it gets worse. The Goldman Sachs report also reveals that under the guise of preventing "illicit activity," the central bankers have decided against fully anonymous accounts and/or have capped the amount of money one can handle anonymously.

> The European Central Bank (ECB) for instance, is considering **imposing balance limits** that forbid people from saving more money than the ECB wants them to save.[41]

They also want to know how people spend their money. In May 2023, the European Union declared that cash payments of 7,000 euros or more are illegal. And in France and Italy, cash payments over 1,000 euros are prohibited.

That same spring, ECB President Christine Lagarde accidentally revealed that Europe's Central Bank would become even nosier when they issue a CBDC.

In March 2023, an undercover journalist posed as Ukraine President Volodymyr Zelensky in a phone call with Lagarde.[42]

During that conversation, which was recorded and later posted to social media, Lagarde revealed that the European Central Bank believes it "could be dangerous" if the European Central Bank were not able to spy on and "control" even the smallest consumer purchases.

> "We are considering whether for very small amounts, anything that is around €300 [or] €400, we could have a mechanism where there is zero control, but that could be dangerous,"[43] Lagarde told the undercover journalist.

In an April 2024 speech to an EU House panel, Klaas Knot, president of the Dutch central bank, admitted that "there will be a holding limit on digital euro [the EU's CBDC] holdings."[44] In other words, **the EU government will dictate how much digital money you will be allowed to have, hold, and use**.

Knot also revealed that each citizen's "personal data must be accessible to an intermediary such as a bank, who must collect and verify it." This invasion of privacy is necessary, he says, to prevent "money laundering and financial terrorism."

The Dutch central banker might as well have used the tired old tyrant's adage: "*You have nothing to fear if you've done nothing wrong.*"

CHAPTER 5

THE CENTRAL BANKERS' CENTRAL BANKS

Many proponents claim these central bank digital currencies are necessary to keep up with technology, as well as China's moves on the international monetary system. But experts warn the true reasons are far more sinister.

> "At its core, a CBDC is about **further centralizing the supply of money in the government**,"
>
> says Norbert Michel, Vice President and Director of the Cato Institute's Center for Monetary and Financial Alternatives.
>
> "It is not about competing with the private sector, or merely giving people another payment option."[45]

"It is about keeping up with technology only in the sense that governments are scared to death of losing control over the money supply to decentralized digital money," Michel continued. "The problem, though, is that a CBDC centralizes the supply of money in a way autocratic governments have only dreamed about in the past." The preeminent central banks have been clear on their views.

INTERNATIONAL MONETARY FUND (IMF)

Speaking at an IMF/World Bank Annual meeting in 2022, **the IMF's Deputy Managing Director Bo Li** told attendees:

> "CBDC can allow government agencies and private sector players to program...targeted policy functions. By programming a CBDC, money can be precisely targeted for what people can own and what [people can do.]"[46]

To be clear, Li was not issuing a warning. Rather, he was extolling this government control of finances as a benefit. The IMF is not a central bank, per se. Instead, it's more like the mother of all central banks. That's because the IMF is an agency of the United Nations.

*As such, it advises the central banks of all U.N. member countries. By the way, before becoming the United Nations' IMF deputy director, Bo Li served as deputy director of the **People's Bank of China**.*

Now, this card-carrying member of the Chinese Communist Party is in charge of telling U.N. members' central banks (like America's Federal Reserve) what to do.

BANK FOR INTERNATIONAL SETTLEMENTS

The Bank for International Settlements (BIS) knows a thing or two about using money to control people.

> *The BIS was established in 1930 via an intergovernmental agreement among the United States, France, Belgium, Great Britain, Italy, Japan, and Germany to facilitate the heavy war reparations imposed on Germany after World War I.*[47]
>
> **The BIS wound up laundering the gold that Nazis yanked from Jewish teeth** *before becoming the central bank to all other central banks.*

> In 1939, when Hitler invaded Czechoslovakia, the BIS transferred Czechoslovakia's entire gold reserves, 23 tons (1.285 billion in today's dollars),[48] directly to Adolf Hitler's Nazi regime.

In fact, throughout the war, the BIS board was comprised of American, British, and French bankers who worked hand in hand with prominent Nazis, many of whom were later convicted of "crimes against humanity" at The Hague.

For instance, Emil Puhl, the Nazi officer in charge of "processing" the dental gold that flowed in from the concentration camps, served on the BIS board throughout the war, as did multiple other Nazi Party officials.

Fast-forward to the present, and the BIS is wholly owned and operated by the central banks it serves, 63 central banks that control 95% of the world's gross domestic product.[49]

The BIS states that its mission is "to support central banks' pursuit of monetary and financial stability through international cooperation, and to act as a bank for central banks."

In other words, the BIS is truly "the" globalist bank—and like its WWII board members, it still wants complete control over humanity.

Speaking in 2021, BIS head Agustín Carstens **admitted** that Central Bank Digital Currency is a scheme with a dual focus—surveillance and control:

> "In cash, we don't know, for example, who's using a 100-dollar bill today," Carstens said. "We don't know who is using a 1,000-peso bill today.
>
> A key difference with the CBDC is the central bank will have absolute control on the rules and regulations that will determine the use of that expression of central bank liability, and also we will have the technology to enforce that. Those two issues are extremely important and that makes a huge difference with respect to what cash is" (emphasis added).
>
> Gabor Gurbacs, director of digital asset strategy at VanEck, responded via social media on July 8, 2021, saying, "The problem with that [Carstens'] statement is that no one hired central banks for a mandate to have 'absolute control' over money and dictate our individual transactions.
>
> It's not within their charter. It's not their job or anyone else's, as a matter of fact. It's not what the people want either."[50]

SWIFT

While the BIS serves as the Central Bankers' bank and regulator, the Society for Worldwide Interbank Financial Communication (SWIFT) is the toolkit used to make BIS members' cross-border payments possible. SWIFT created multiple programs and tools that transmit "messages containing the payment instructions between financial institutions involved in a transaction"[51]

Founded in 1973, SWIFT was established to prevent a private entity headquartered in the United States from having too much power over international transactions. Prior to that time, international transactions were largely governed by the First National City Bank of New York, which went on to become CitiBank.[52]

At its core, SWIFT is a behemoth of an electronic communication system used by world banks to facilitate the transfer of money across international borders. To be clear, SWIFT is not a bank, and it does not store or handle cash. Instead, it is the go-between that allows (or prevents) international financial transactions to be processed[53] and bankers to make a profit.

SWIFT is owned and operated by the world's largest banks and central bankers. Headquartered in Belgium, SWIFT is "overseen" by the central banks of the G10 (Group of 10, though it is now 11) nations, which are Belgium, Canada, France, Germany, Italy, Japan, the Netherlands, Sweden, Switzerland, the United Kingdom, and the United States.[54]

In 2012, the group of overseers was expanded to include the central banks of Argentina, Australia, Brazil, China, Hong Kong, India, Saudi Arabia, Indonesia, Korea, Mexico, Russia, Saudi Arabia, Singapore, South Africa, Spain and Turkey. SWIFT says this expansion of the Oversight Forum was necessary to provide "a forum for the G-10 central banks to share information on Swift oversight activities with a wider group of central banks."

> In the 50 years since SWIFT was formed, it has grown to govern more than 11,000 banks in over 200 countries, effectively making SWIFT a global messenger and controller of world financial transactions.

Every three years, SWIFT adjusts its leadership by putting the bankers with the highest volume of financial transactions on its board of directors and in charge of decision-making.[55]

As of May 2024, SWIFT's board of directors is comprised of:

JPMorgan Chase, chair, Lloyd's Bank of London, deputy chair, Bank of China, Banque Nationale de Paris Paribas of France, Banque Populaire Caisse d'Epargne of France, Citibank of New York, Clearstream of Luxembourg, Commerzbank of Germany and Poland, Commonwealth Bank of Australia, Deutsche Bank of Germany, Euroclear of Belgium, FirstRand of South Africa, HSBC of London, ING of the Netherlands, Intesa Sanpaolo of Italy, KBC of Belgium, MUFG of Japan, NatWest of London, Nordea of Finland, Royal Bank of Canada, Santander of Spain, SEB of Sweden, UBS of Switzerland, and the Association of Banks in Singapore.[56]

Needless to say, these money handlers have a vested interest in ensuring continued control over the world's finances. The SWIFT member nations' central bank governors and finance ministers meet in conjunction with the International Monetary Fund and World Bank annual meetings to decide financial and monetary policies for the global economy.

In recent years, SWIFT has effectively turned into an arm of the U.S. State Department, enforcing the State Department's will on other countries, primarily through sanctions. Getting kicked out of SWIFT has traditionally been a death knell to a country's entire economy because the people, businesses, and governments of the alienated countries are no longer able to send or receive money internationally.[57]

A recent report by the *New York Federal Reserve*[58] explains that SWIFT is an important tool in enforcing sanctions against governments and people.

In the section entitled, "*The Role of SWIFT in the Implementation of Financial Sanctions,*" the Fed explains that sanctioned countries are prohibited from using the SWIFT system, cutting them off from the world's most commonly used vehicle for international money transfers.

The Federal Reserve paper relays the history:

> *In February 2012, the United States passed the* **Iran Sanctions, Accountability, and Human Rights Act of 2012***, authorizing the US president to impose sanctions on persons or institutions that provided financial messaging services to designated Iranian financial institution, including SWIFT.*
>
> *As a response to the US legislation, SWIFT announced the decision to discontinue access to designated Iranian financial institutions as soon as it had clarity from the European Union.*
>
> *On March 15, 2012, the European Union passed* **EU Regulation 267/2012** *forbidding SWIFT from providing financial messaging services to some EU-sanctioned Iranian banks, including Iran's central bank. SWIFT complied with this regulation and disconnected the EU-sanctioned Iranian banks from its system.*

In 2014, the U.S. government used the same formula to sanction not only the Russian government, but also Russian individuals, over the country's decision to invade Crimea. The U.S. government added yet more sanctions after Russia invaded Ukraine, this time adding sanctions against Russian banks. SWIFT enforced the sanctions every time.

In early May 2024, SWIFT announced it was testing a CBDC transaction system with 38 commercial and central bankers.[59] The result of this experiment will be a global umbrella, built by central bankers, to manage the movement of all CBDCs around the world.

> In other words, **like Sauron's "One Ring to rule them all"** in *The Lord of the Rings* **epic trilogy,** SWIFT aims to have one CBDC system that governs the movement (and use) of all CBDCs throughout the world.

SWIFT claims the move to CBDCs is necessary to enable cheaper, faster inter-national payments.[60] But instant, free, or low-fee international monetary transfers are *already* available via cryptocurrencies like Bitcoin. So why are they bothering at all?

According to Reuters, 90% of the world's central bankers are investigating and/or developing CBDCs because they "don't want to be left behind by bitcoin."[61]

Actually Bitcoin totally upended globalists' ability to control and profit off of the world's international commerce and monetary transactions. Terrified of losing their grip and massive profits, as well as the ability to punish and sanction political enemies, globalists are now scrambling to salvage their power position.

> **CBDC backers want CONTROL.**
> And not just Joe Biden- or Gavin Newsom-type of make-you-stay-at-home and close-your-church controls, but GLOBAL control over every cent earned, stored, and sent worldwide by governments AND their citizens—**including YOU!**

The ultimate goal is to ensure that no one is able to buy or sell without the globalist central banker's permission and oversight.

ABSOLUTE CONTROL IS THE END GAME

Like the Chinese Communist Party, the globalists believe that they, not you, know what is best for your life and your finances. And they are willing to go to any length to impose their control upon your life.

"If governments and central banks control the creation, distribution, and exchange of virtual money, whatever remains of free markets will disappear," says Gatestone Institute writer J.B. Shurk.[62]

Shurk notes that CBDCs allow the government to control the creation, distribution, and exchange of all currency, which will be the death knell of free markets and private property rights.

> *"If governments and central banks maintain a digital monopoly over the only legalized forms of money, then they may redistribute wealth or penalize personal behavior without regard for individual rights or limits to their control,"* Shurk says.

The European Parliament report on CBDC also recommends sharing citizen spending data with "financial intelligence units," in case of terrorism, of course.

IMF's former chief of financial studies, Eswar Prasad, has tipped the hand of the globalists seeking a cashless society. In a 2021 interview, Prasad—who supports CBDCs—gave a chilling look at how our government could use our own personal money against us.

"One should recognize that the CBDC creates new opportunity for monetary policy. If we all had CBDC accounts instead of cash, in principle it might be possible to implement negative interest rates simply by shrinking balances in CBDC accounts," Prasad says.[63]

"In other words," says CATO Institute's Norbert Michel, "central banks will take money *out* of people's accounts to conduct monetary policy."[64]

> Natalie Smolenski, senior adviser at the Bitcoin Policy Institute and executive director of the Texas Bitcoin Foundation, explains it a different way:
>
> "The objective of imposing negative interest rates," says Smolenski, is to **"prevent recessions by stimulating near-tern consumer spending,"** which is **"achieved at the cost of accelerating the destruction of private wealth"**
>
> (emphasis added).

Given Prasad's pro-government control perspective, perhaps it is no surprise to learn that Prasad, too, has a connection to Communist China. Prasad previously served as the head of the IMF's China division.[65]

Monetary scholars agree that CBDCs increase government interference into **YOUR** finances, including dictating how much cash you are allowed to have. The Bahamas, which already launched its CBDC, has instituted such cash limits on its citizens.

"At its core, this brave new world of monetary policy equates to the government saying that your money isn't really your money," Michel says. "Your property rights are subservient to the 'public good' and the supposed necessity of 'managing the national economy.'...The truth is CBDCs are government's attempt to protect its privileged position and exert more control over people's money."[66]

Smolenski cautions, "A CBDC could be programmed to only be spendable at certain retailers or service providers, at certain times, by certain people. The government could maintain lists of 'preferred providers' to encourage spending with certain companies over others and 'discouraged providers' to punish spending with others"[67] (emphasis added).

> *Sweden seems to be taking Prasad's recommendation. The Nordic country is also considering limiting how much money citizens can have and use. To ensure compliance, Sweden has explored implementing negative interest rates[68] through which Swedish citizens will be charged for having too much money in their savings account.*

> In Israel, residents are "allowed" to have 1,000 shekels (about $275 U.S.) to spend "privately" without being tracked under the Jewish state's newly issued CBDC.[69]

In India, where the Indian CBDC is already in effect, there is no privacy at all.[70] The Indian government is considering allowing citizens to "delete" a certain number of transactions from their accounts. However, the transactions are only deleted commercially, meaning the government can still see the transaction.

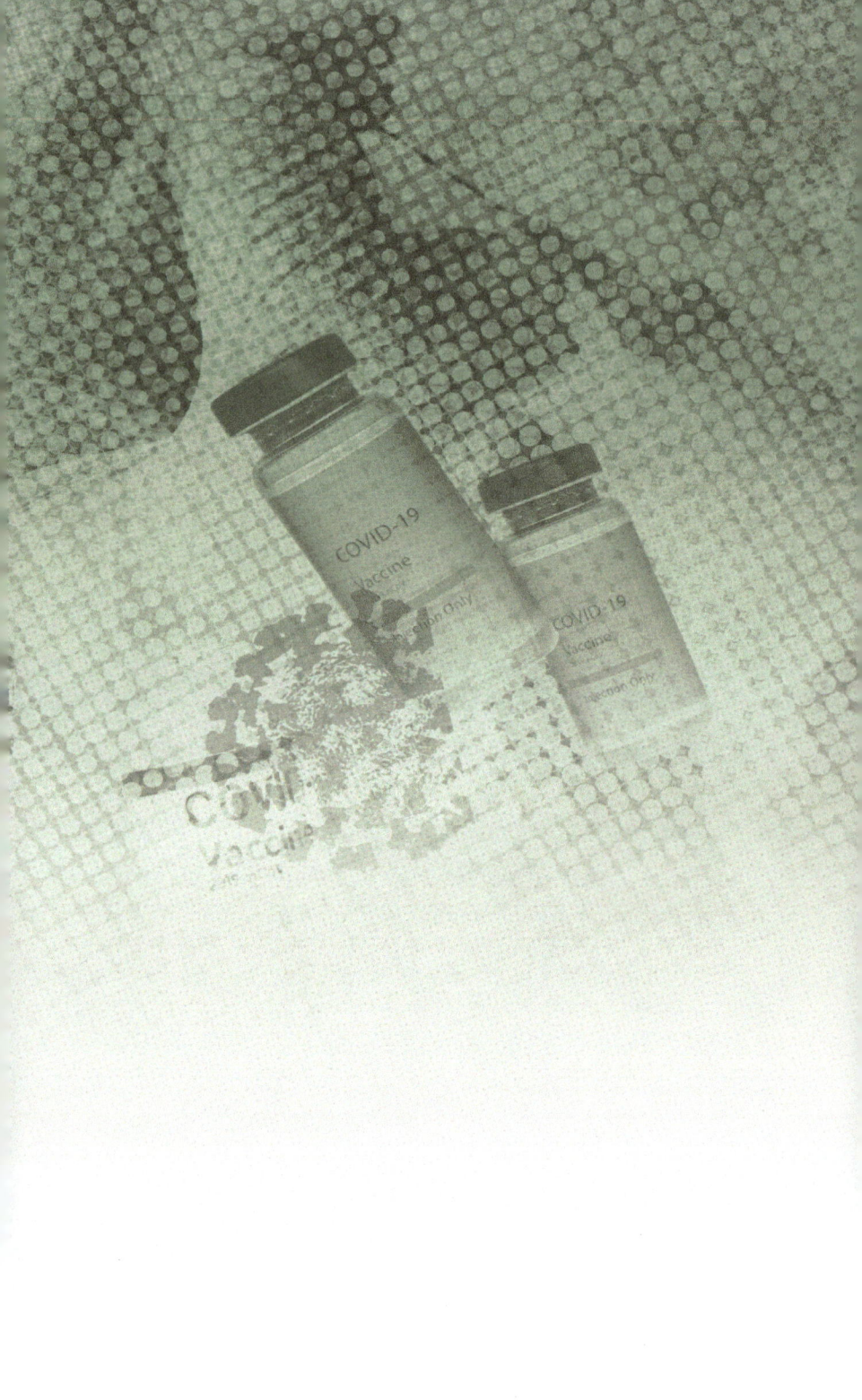

CHAPTER 6

PAST IS PROLOGUE

Beyond speculation, we already know what the controllers have already said and done. For decades, the progressive left has systematically taken steps attempting to control how people are allowed to use their own money. The most memorable example is New York City Mayor Michael Bloomberg's 2012 ban on large sodas,[71] and the New York City Health Department debated banning large movie theater popcorn buckets.[72]

The Obama-Biden administration used the Internal Revenue Service and other government agencies to attack Tea Party activists whom they viewed as a political threat. That same administration tried to force 501(c)(1) nonprofits (corporations organized under an act of Congress that are exempt from federal income tax) to disclose their donors in an effort to scare people away from supporting those groups.

During the COVID shutdowns, freedom-loving individuals were held hostage by government agencies and agents that sought to dictate if, where, and how Americans could eat, shop, and worship.

Tyrants of all levels went into overtime exercising newly invented powers to punish those who dared defy the regime's unconstitutional orders and radical ideology.

Los Angeles Mayor Eric Garcetti threatened to cut off power and water to Pastor John MacArthur's Grace Community Church because members refused to stop attending services during CA Gov. Gavin Newsom's unconstitutional shutdown decree.[73]

Chicago Mayor Lori Lightfoot threatened to seize and destroy our client Elim Romanian Pentecostal Church's property and buildings if more than 10 people dared to meet in the church's 1,300-seat sanctuary.

Police helicopters descended upon our client Pastor Rodney Howard-Browne's residence, arresting him in the early morning hours in front of his wife and children. His "crime" was refusing to stop The River Church's greenhouse and food pantry program, which fed 900 impoverished families a week during the COVID shutdowns.

On Easter Sunday 2020, every member who attended our client Maryville Baptist Church of Kentucky's drive-in, stay-in-your-car Easter parking lot service was put on two-week house arrest, causing them to lose their jobs in the middle of an economic crisis.

Furthermore, the Biden/Harris administration has already used American taxpayer dollars to force media companies to silence and censor Christians and medical professionals who refused to toe disgraced Dr. Anthony Fauci's unscientific, and long-proven dangerous, demands.

Had a CBDC been in place during COVID, the tyrants' jobs would have been much easier. A simple push of a button by the Federal Reserve would have cut off each of these churches' and individuals' access to their own money.

In October 2021, the Biden administration demanded the federal government be allowed full access to any bank account that transacted $600 or more a year.[74] **That's an average of just $50 a month!**

In effect, the administration was demanding to view the personal finances of teenagers who mow lawns for extra spending money.

Thankfully, after a massive public outcry, the administration was forced to back down from its invasive financial surveillance scheme.[75] However, a CBDC would make the federal government every citizen's immediate banker. As such, the feds need not obtain a warrant to view citizens' financial transactions. They need only pull up each person's federal government-issued digital currency account to see and control every single penny earned or spent.

Throughout the COVID "crisis," we saw firsthand how eager officials were to erase liberty. With the progressive left's insistence on shoving earth-polluting electric cars on the American public, it's not hard to imagine Nancy Pelosi, Alexandria Ocasio-Cortez, and similar cohorts from limiting your ability to purchase good old-fashioned gasoline.

In fact, the world's preeminent CBDC development group has already admitted that this is the plan.

> **Dr. Raoul Herborg** *is the managing director at G+D, a company that creates Central Bank Digital Currencies for countries around the globe. Lately, it seems Mr. Herborg's primary job is to convince you that all the financial spying and controls inherent to a CBDC are "benefits" we should embrace.*

When asked, "What CBDC use cases are you most excited about and why?" in a recent interview, Dr. Herborg responded, in part, "CBDC smart wallets could be used to promote national policies that help meet sustainability objectives, e.g., by issuing a 'green' wallet. This would act as an incentive for consumers to buy environmentally friendly products and services."[76]

Herborg's response is telling. He is marketing government dictation of how people spend their money as a feature and benefit of CBDCs, ignoring the obvious and outrageous tyrannies to be imposed on how the consumer is allowed to use their own hard-earned money.

The concept of a "green wallet" sounds lovely, I'm sure, to "climate change" fanatics. But as we have seen with such activists from former Vice President Al Gore to Sen. Elizabeth Warren, "rules" are for us and not for them. They insist on flying gas-guzzling private jets to their massive estates around the globe while demanding average people lower their thermostats, take public transportation, and be shuffled into "15-minute cities."

Herberg's company touts a host of other CBDC "benefits" as well, including:

- *Central banks would be able to define policy rules that apply to all wallets—and cannot be changed...including the fact that the central banks can* **limit the amount that can be held in any single wallet**" *(emphasis added).*

- *Companies would be able to program CBDCs to dictate how employees are allowed to use their own paychecks, including programming portions of the paycheck* "**solely for use by a company's employees for the purchase of healthy food.**" *In other words, no potato chips or Big Gulps for you!*

Joe Biden's executive order confirms Herborg's statements. The last line in Section I of the order states that the government intends to use CBDCs to address: "Human rights; financial inclusion and equity; and climate change and pollution."

These open admissions reveal that CBDC proponents believe it is imperative that consumers be forced into government-dictated behaviors. Such a concept is diametrically opposed to individual responsibility and freedom.

A CBDC in the hands of government spells doom for American liberty. Suddenly, politicians and government agents won't simply "suggest" you follow their increasingly bizarre policies like replacing beef with bug protein or buying electric cars whose batteries poison the earth.

With a CBDC, the government will be able to dictate these decisions by preventing you from using your own money to buy a steak or a tank of gas.

But it's not just the politicians we need to fear. The U.S. government's central bank, the Federal Reserve, poses every bit as much danger to American citizens' finances.

> For decades, the New York Federal Reserve's (Fed's) "Doomsday Book" has been held in secret. The book contains the NY Fed's guiding principles and reveals an **unelected, unaccountable globalist cabal** that believes it need not be bound by the whims of Congress, nor by the law.
>
> Instead, the NY Fed believes it can justify **any "emergency action"** the board dreams up.

Emre Kuvvet, a professor of finance at Nova Southeastern University, recently managed to get his hands on a copy of the New York Federal Reserve's "Doomsday Book," and its contents are disturbing.

The book lays out the history of the NY Fed's decision-making processes and justifications for action.

"Instead of adhering strictly to clear legislative boundaries to justify its actions during financial crises, the central bank appears to ground many of its decisions in the New York Fed's belief in the Fed's discretionary authority," says Kuvvet. "It relies on precedent for many of its actions, *without explicit congressional authorization* in some instances." [77]

"This approach implies that establishing clear legislative boundaries for the Fed might be a futile endeavor because the central bank—or at least the legal team at its dominant member bank—apparently believes it can rely on precedent to justify virtually any emergency action," says Kuvvet, (emphasis added).

"This finding is of prime concern when questions loom around the Federal Reserve's authority to issue a CBDC," says Nicholas Anthony, policy analyst at Cato Institute.[78]

"Although some argue the Federal Reserve Act clearly prohibits individuals from holding accounts at the central bank, it shouldn't be forgotten that the Fed based its CBDC discussion paper on an intermediated CBDC that would involve putting financial institutions in the middle of the process—*effectively creating a legal gray area.*

Based on Mr. Kuvvet's findings, Congress shouldn't wait to establish clear and enforceable boundaries," Anthony concludes.

"[N]ew monetary systems risk being swept in without any democratic oversight at all," according to *Financial Times* analyst Izabella Kaminska. This is important because CBDCs have the power to radically change our entire economy, giving broad powers to unelected Federal Reserve central bankers. Whether by design or default, those broad powers are designed to control your money, and therefore your freedom."[79]

On May 4, 2022, Fed Chair Jerome Powell admitted that the Federal Reserve believes their main job is to "keep wages down" in order to keep the economy on track.[80] In other words, keeping people poor is apparently part of the master plan.

In addition, the MIT report on the "Project Hamilton" collaboration with the Boston Fed reveals something equally chilling. The report notes that the project's primary purpose was to see if the Fed's CBDC digital dollar program worked at all.

> *The "secondary goal," according to MIT, was to "create a platform" for "data gathering," i.e., spying on every single financial transaction made anywhere by anyone. It is no longer enough for the Fed to keep your hourly pay or salary low. Now they want to know when, where, and how you earn, store, and spend every single cent you make.*

> The combination of these factors reveals the central banker's two aims— (1) keeping you poor (and therefore dependent upon government largesse) and (2) keeping you under the globalists' centralized control.

Recent U.S. administrations have been ever more willing to allow the United Nations and its sub-agency, the World Health Organization (WHO) to dictate domestic policies.

If the U.N. and WHO wish to enforce their travel restrictions, a globalist-minded U.S. presidential administration could easily use a CBDC to prevent individuals from using their own money to travel, or buying supplements and medicines the WHO doesn't like.

Furthermore, if the U.N. and WHO double down on their "sustainability" agenda to replace meat with cricket flour, a CBDC can be used to prevent Americans from paying a farmer for a side of beef or even a steak.

And because a CBDC is designed to replace and eventually eliminate cash, Americans will have no other choice but to comply. Put simply, a CBDC would be the single largest assault on financial autonomy and privacy in history.

> "A fully implemented CBDC gives the government complete control over the money going into and coming out of every person's account,"
>
> says Michel of the Cato Institute.

> "It's not difficult to see that this level of government control is incompatible with both economic and political freedom."

PROPAGANDA ON THE RISE

Big-government control-minded propagandists like Paul Krugman are already trying to paint anyone who opposes the Fed's CBDC scheme as a criminal. In recent comments to the press, Krugman insisted that opposition to the CBDC would "protect the ability of wiseguys to evade taxes, launder money, buy and sell illegal drugs, and engage in extortion."

Krugman—whose globalist economic theories played a large part in moving American manufacturing jobs offshore,[81] thereby impoverishing the middle class[82]—wants you to believe that only bad guys oppose the CBDC, and that if you aren't a criminal, you don't have anything to hide from the government.

But such an argument belies our constitutional rights, not the least of which is to be secure in our papers and documents and in the daily transactions of our lives without snooping or interference from power-hungry bureaucrats and tyrannical politicians.

> **Friedrich Hayek**, *an economist whose theories on individual property (including money) better align with the Constitution, argues that liberty is only possible when an individual has full ownership of and control over his possessions, his land, and the work of his hands without government interference or control over those resources.*

> **Robert P. Murphy**, *an economist and senior fellow with Mises Institute, says the Fed would not even need to officially launch a so-called "FedCoin" to start its CBDC financial surveillance scheme. Instead, "it would just take people switching their checking accounts to the Fed."*[83]

If "people's checking deposits were liabilities on the Fed's balance sheet, that would be a central bank digital currency," Murphy said. "They would still be 'dollars,' it's just that the Fed would be in complete control; there wouldn't be an intermediate level of private—and competing!—commercial banks."

In other words, according to Murphy and several other liberty-minded economists, "If average Americans hold bank accounts directly with the Fed, its control over their lives would be nearly absolute, particularly if cash is phased out."

The Cato Institute says, "a CBDC would most likely be the single largest assault on financial privacy since the creation of the Bank Secrecy Act and the establishment of the third-party doctrine." [84]

The Fed was created in 1913 to stabilize the financial sector. The Great Depression occurred under its watch 16 years later, along with a seemingly never-ending number of financial crises resulting from the Fed's heavy hand on the economic scales—not the least of which is our current skyrocketing inflation and the near complete devaluation of the U.S. dollar.

ECONOMIC FREEDOM: THE BASIS OF LIBERTY

CBDCs seek to control the fruits of your labor—money. The basis of Hayek's theories on economic freedom is found in the principle that people are only truly free when they can freely store and enjoy the fruits of their labors—their money. A government that seeks to limit those freedoms sets its citizens on a sure path to serfdom, via Marxist money.

Like Karl Marx, the globalists' actions speak to the hubris of man and the desire of tyrants to seize control and implement their will over every aspect of life and God's green Earth.

Throughout the Old Testament, we see mankind continually seeking higher powers **OTHER THAN GOD**. They sought judges, then kings, and yet humanity was still a wreck.

The globalists of today think they have all the answers. They think they are smarter than all of us, and they don't believe in God. In fact, they reject God's authority in their lives and in all other lives.

True freedom, including financial freedom, is found **by simply living as God instructs through His Word, the Bible.** But a major part of doing so is protecting the RIGHT to live that way.

Article I, Section 8, Clause 5 of the U.S. Constitution *states that:*

"Congress shall have the power...[t]o coin Money, regulate the Value thereof, and of foreign Coin, and fix the Standard of Weights and Measures."

> The Supreme Court, in *Houston v. Moore*, 18 U.S. 1, 49 (1820) and *Sturges v. Crowninshield*, 17 U.S. 122, 125 (1819), found the federal government, via Congress, has the exclusive power to create, define, and "coin" money.[85]
>
> **Section 31 U.S.C. 5103** *further refines this power and states that "coins, currency, certificates, etc. offered by the Federal Reserve" are legal tender for use anywhere in the U.S. As such, monetary instruments offered by the Federal Reserve cannot be rejected or banned by either state legislatures or merchants.*

Theoretically, that would include CBDCs as well.[86] At present, there is considerable debate as to whether the Federal Reserve or even a U.S. president can implement a CBDC without congressional approval.

To ensure citizens are fully protected from this 21st-century Marxist Money, Congress should go on the immediate offensive, developing and passing legislation to ban retail CBDCs before they can be forced on the American public.

And because tyrannical entities have banned cryptocurrencies like Bitcoin, Congress also should pass legislation preventing the federal government from banning or taking other detrimental action against Bitcoin and other privacy-oriented free market cryptocurrencies.

These measures are necessary to prevent the United States government from adopting the financial surveillance and civilian control measures of tyrants around the globe—including those employed by the Chinese Communist Party.

Let's not be the people who relegate control over our lives to tyrannical rulers who seek to eliminate God, replacing His wisdom with their hubris, and enforcing their will through Central Bank Digital Currencies.

Let's not trade our financial freedom for Marxist Money.

APPENDICES

EXECUTIVE ORDER 14067

By the authority vested in me as President by the Constitution and the laws of the United States of America, it is hereby ordered as follows:

Section 1. *Policy.* Advances in digital and distributed ledger technology for financial services have led to dramatic growth in markets for digital assets, with profound implications for the protection of consumers, investors, and businesses, including data privacy and security; financial stability and systemic risk; crime; national security; the ability to exercise human rights; financial inclusion and equity; and energy demand and climate change. In November 2021, non-state issued digital assets reached a combined market capitalization of $3 trillion, up from approximately $14 billion in early November 2016. Monetary authorities globally are also exploring, and in some cases introducing, central bank digital currencies (CBDCs).

While many activities involving digital assets are within the scope of existing domestic laws and regulations, an area where the United States has been a global leader, growing development and adoption of digital assets and related innovations, as well as inconsistent controls to defend against certain key risks, necessitate an evolution and alignment of the United States Government approach to digital assets. The United States has an interest in responsible financial innovation, expanding access to safe and affordable financial services, and reducing the cost of domestic and cross-border funds transfers and payments, including through the continued modernization of public payment systems. We must take strong steps to reduce the risks that digital assets could pose to consumers, investors, and business protections; financial stability and financial system integrity; combating and preventing crime and illicit finance; national security; the ability to exercise human rights; financial inclusion and equity; and climate change and pollution.

Sec. 2. *Objectives.* The principal policy objectives of the United States with respect to digital assets are as follows:

(a) We must protect consumers, investors, and businesses in the United States. The unique and varied features of digital assets can pose significant financial risks to consumers, investors, and businesses if appropriate protections are not in place.

In the absence of sufficient oversight and standards, firms providing digital asset services may provide inadequate protections for sensitive financial data, custodial and other arrangements relating to customer assets and funds, or disclosures of risks associated with investment. Cybersecurity and market failures at major digital asset exchanges and trading platforms have resulted in billions of dollars in losses. The United States should ensure that safeguards are in place and promote the responsible development of digital assets to protect consumers, investors, and businesses; maintain privacy; and shield against arbitrary or unlawful surveillance, which can contribute to human rights abuses.

(b) We must protect United States and global financial stability and mitigate systemic risk. Some digital asset trading platforms and service providers have grown rapidly in size and complexity and may not be subject to or in compliance with appropriate regulations or supervision. Digital asset issuers, exchanges and trading platforms, and intermediaries whose activities may increase risks to financial stability, should, as appropriate, be subject to and in compliance with regulatory and supervisory standards that govern traditional market infrastructures and financial firms, in line with the general principle of "same business, same risks, same rules." The new and unique uses and functions that digital assets can facilitate may create additional economic and financial risks requiring an evolution to a regulatory approach that adequately addresses those risks.

(c) We must mitigate the illicit finance and national security risks posed by misuse of digital assets. Digital assets may pose significant illicit finance risks, including money laundering, cybercrime and ransomware, narcotics and human trafficking, and terrorism and proliferation financing.

Digital assets may also be used as a tool to circumvent United States and foreign financial sanctions regimes and other tools and authorities.

Further, while the United States has been a leader in setting international standards for the regulation and supervision of digital assets for anti-money laundering and countering the financing of terrorism (AML/CFT), poor or nonexistent implementation of those standards in some jurisdictions abroad can present significant illicit financing risks for the United States and global financial systems.

Illicit actors, including the perpetrators of ransomware incidents and other cybercrime, often launder and cash out of their illicit proceeds using digital asset service providers in jurisdictions that have not yet effectively implemented the international standards set by the inter-governmental Financial Action Task Force (FATF). The continued availability of service providers in jurisdictions where international AML/CFT standards are not effectively implemented enables financial activity without illicit finance controls. Growth in decentralized financial ecosystems, peer-to-peer payment activity, and obscured blockchain ledgers without controls to mitigate illicit finance could also present additional market and national security risks in the future.

The United States must ensure appropriate controls and accountability for current and future digital assets systems to promote high standards for transparency, privacy, and security—including through regulatory, governance, and technological measures—that counter illicit activities and preserve or enhance the efficacy of our national security tools. When digital assets are abused or used in illicit ways, or undermine national security, it is in the national interest to take actions to mitigate these illicit finance and national security risks through regulation, oversight, law enforcement action, or use of other United States Government authorities.

(d) We must reinforce United States leadership in the global financial system and in technological and economic competitiveness, including through the responsible development of payment innovations and digital assets. The United States has an interest in ensuring that it remains at the forefront of responsible development and design of digital assets and the technology that underpins new forms of payments and capital flows in the international financial system, particularly in setting standards that promote: democratic values; the rule of law; privacy; the protection of consumers, investors, and businesses; and interoperability with digital platforms, legacy architecture, and international payment systems.

The United States derives significant economic and national security benefits from the central role that the United States dollar and United States financial institutions and markets play in the global financial system. Continued United States leadership in the global financial system will sustain United States financial power and promote United States economic interests.

(e) We must promote access to safe and affordable financial services. Many Americans are underbanked and the costs of cross-border money transfers and payments are high. The United States has a strong interest in promoting responsible innovation that expands equitable access to financial services, particularly for those Americans underserved by the traditional banking system, including by making investments and domestic and cross-border funds transfers and payments cheaper, faster, and safer, and by promoting greater and more cost-efficient access to financial products and services. The United States also has an interest in ensuring that the benefits of financial innovation are enjoyed equitably by all Americans and that any disparate impacts of financial innovation are mitigated.

(f) We must support technological advances that promote responsible development and use of digital assets. The technological architecture of different digital assets has substantial implications for privacy, national security, the operational security and resilience of financial systems, climate change, the ability to exercise human rights, and other national goals.

The United States has an interest in ensuring that digital asset technologies and the digital payments ecosystem are developed, designed, and implemented in a responsible manner that includes privacy and security in their architecture, integrates features and controls that defend against illicit exploitation, and reduces negative climate impacts and environmental pollution, as may result from some cryptocurrency mining.

Sec. 3. *Coordination.* The Assistant to the President for National Security Affairs (APNSA) and the Assistant to the President for Economic Policy (APEP) shall coordinate, through the interagency process described in National Security Memorandum 2 of February 4, 2021 (Renewing the National Security Council System), the executive branch actions necessary to implement this order.

The interagency process shall include, as appropriate: the Secretary of State, the Secretary of the Treasury, the Secretary of Defense, the Attorney General, the Secretary of Commerce, the Secretary of Labor, the Secretary of Energy, the Secretary of Homeland Security, the Administrator of the Environmental Protection Agency, the Director of the Office of Management and Budget, the Director of National Intelligence, the Director of the Domestic Policy Council, the Chair of the Council of Economic Advisers, the Director of the Office of Science and Technology Policy, the Administrator of the Office of Information and Regulatory Affairs, the Director of the National Science Foundation, and the Administrator of the United States Agency for International Development.

Representatives of other executive departments and agencies (agencies) and other senior officials may be invited to attend interagency meetings as appropriate, including, with due respect for their regulatory independence, representatives of the Board of Governors of the Federal Reserve System, the Consumer Financial Protection Bureau (CFPB), the Federal Trade Commission (FTC), the Securities and Exchange Commission (SEC), the Commodity Futures Trading Commission (CFTC), the Federal Deposit Insurance Corporation, the Office of the Comptroller of the Currency, and other Federal regulatory agencies.

Sec. 4. *Policy* and Actions Related to United States Central Bank Digital Currencies. (a) The policy of my Administration on a United States CBDC is as follows:

(i) Sovereign money is at the core of a well-functioning financial system, macroeconomic stabilization policies, and economic growth. My Administration places the highest urgency on research and development efforts into the potential design and deployment options of a United States CBDC. These efforts should include assessments of possible benefits and risks for consumers, investors, and businesses; financial stability and systemic risk; payment systems; national security; the ability to exercise human rights; financial inclusion and equity; and the actions required to launch a United States CBDC if doing so is deemed to be in the national interest.

(ii) My Administration sees merit in showcasing United States leadership and participation in international fora related to CBDCs and in multi-country conversations and pilot projects involving CBDCs.

Any future dollar payment system should be designed in a way that is consistent with United States priorities (as outlined in section 4(a)(i) of this order) and democratic values, including privacy protections, and that ensures the global financial system has appropriate transparency, connectivity, and platform and architecture interoperability or transferability, as appropriate.

(iii) A United States CBDC may have the potential to support efficient and low-cost transactions, particularly for cross-border funds transfers and payments, and to foster greater access to the financial system, with fewer of the risks posed by private sector-administered digital assets.

A United States CBDC that is interoperable with CBDCs issued by other monetary authorities could facilitate faster and lower-cost cross-border payments and potentially boost economic growth, support the continued centrality of the United States within the international financial system, and help to protect the unique role that the dollar plays in global finance.

There are also, however, potential risks and downsides to consider. We should prioritize timely assessments of potential benefits and risks under various designs to ensure that the United States remains a leader in the international financial system.

(b) Within 180 days of the date of this order, the Secretary of the Treasury, in consultation with the Secretary of State, the Attorney General, the Secretary of Commerce, the Secretary of Homeland Security, the Director of the Office of Management and Budget, the Director of National Intelligence, and the heads of other relevant agencies, shall submit to the President a report on the future of money and payment systems, including the conditions that drive broad adoption of digital assets; the extent to which technological innovation may influence these outcomes; and the implications for the United States financial system, the modernization of and changes to payment systems, economic growth, financial inclusion, and national security. This report shall be coordinated through the interagency process described in section 3 of this order. Based on the potential United States CBDC design options, this report shall include an analysis of:

(i) the potential implications of a United States CBDC, based on the possible design choices, for national interests, including implications for economic growth and stability;

(ii) the potential implications a United States CBDC might have on financial inclusion;

(iii) the potential relationship between a CBDC and private sector administered digital assets;

(iv) the future of sovereign and privately produced money globally and implications for our financial system and democracy;

(v) the extent to which foreign CBDCs could displace existing currencies and alter the payment system in ways that could undermine United States financial centrality;

(vi) the potential implications for national security and financial crime, including an analysis of illicit financing risks, sanctions risks, other law enforcement and national security interests, and implications for human rights; and

(vii) an assessment of the effects that the growth of foreign CBDCs may have on United States interests generally.

(c) The Chairman of the Board of Governors of the Federal Reserve System (Chairman of the Federal Reserve) is encouraged to continue to research and report on the extent to which CBDCs could improve the efficiency and reduce the costs of existing and future payments systems, to continue to assess the optimal form of a United States CBDC, and to develop a strategic plan for Federal Reserve and broader United States Government action, as appropriate, that evaluates the necessary steps and requirements for the potential implementation and launch of a United States CBDC. The Chairman of the Federal Reserve is also encouraged to evaluate the extent to which a United States CBDC, based on the potential design options, could enhance or impede the ability of monetary policy to function effectively as a critical macroeconomic stabilization tool.

(d) The Attorney General, in consultation with the Secretary of the Treasury and the Chairman of the Federal Reserve, shall:

(i) within 180 days of the date of this order, provide to the President through the APNSA and APEP an assessment of whether legislative changes would be necessary to issue a United States CBDC, should it be deemed appropriate and in the national interest; and

(ii) within 210 days of the date of this order, provide to the President through the APNSA and the APEP a corresponding legislative proposal, based on consideration of the report submitted by the Secretary of the Treasury under section 4(b) of this order and any materials developed by the Chairman of the Federal Reserve consistent with section 4(c) of this order.

Sec. 5. *Measures to Protect Consumers, Investors, and Businesses.* (a) The increased use of digital assets and digital asset exchanges and trading platforms may increase the risks of crimes such as fraud and theft, other statutory and regulatory violations, privacy and data breaches, unfair and abusive acts or practices, and other cyber incidents faced by consumers, investors, and businesses. The rise in use of digital assets, and differences across communities, may also present disparate financial risk to less informed market participants or exacerbate inequities. It is critical to ensure that digital assets do not pose undue risks to consumers, investors, or businesses, and to put in place protections as a part of efforts to expand access to safe and affordable financial services.

(b) Consistent with the goals stated in section 5(a) of this order:

(i) Within 180 days of the date of this order, the Secretary of the Treasury, in consultation with the Secretary of Labor and the heads of other relevant agencies, including, as appropriate, the heads of independent regulatory agencies such as the FTC, the SEC, the CFTC, Federal banking agencies, and the CFPB, shall submit to the President a report, or section of the report required by section 4 of this order, on the implications of developments and adoption of digital assets and changes in financial market and payment system infrastructures for United States consumers, investors, businesses, and for equitable economic growth.

One section of the report shall address the conditions that would drive mass adoption of different types of digital assets and the risks and opportunities such growth might present to United States consumers, investors, and businesses, including a focus on how technological innovation may impact these efforts and with an eye toward those most vulnerable to disparate impacts.

The report shall also include policy recommendations, including potential regulatory and legislative actions, as appropriate, to protect United States consumers, investors, and businesses, and support expanding access to safe and affordable financial services. The report shall be coordinated through the interagency process described in section 3 of this order.

(ii) Within 180 days of the date of this order, the Director of the Office of Science and Technology Policy and the Chief Technology Officer of the United States, in consultation with the Secretary of the Treasury, the Chairman of the Federal Reserve, and the heads of other relevant agencies, shall submit to the President a technical evaluation of the technological infrastructure, capacity, and expertise that would be necessary at relevant agencies to facilitate and support the introduction of a CBDC system should one be proposed. The evaluation should specifically address the technical risks of the various designs, including with respect to emerging and future technological developments, such as quantum computing. The evaluation should also include any reflections or recommendations on how the inclusion of digital assets in Federal processes may affect the work of the United States Government and the provision of Government services, including risks and benefits to cybersecurity, customer experience, and social-safety-net programs. The evaluation shall be coordinated through the interagency process described in section 3 of this order.

(iii) Within 180 days of the date of this order, the Attorney General, in consultation with the Secretary of the Treasury and the Secretary of Homeland Security, shall submit to the President a report on the role of law enforcement agencies in detecting, investigating, and prosecuting criminal activity related to digital assets. The report shall include any recommendations on regulatory or legislative actions, as appropriate.

(iv) The Attorney General, the Chair of the FTC, and the Director of the CFPB are each encouraged to consider what, if any, effects the growth of digital assets could have on competition policy.

(v) The Chair of the FTC and the Director of the CFPB are each encouraged to consider the extent to which privacy or consumer protection measures within their respective jurisdictions may be used to protect users of digital assets and whether additional measures may be needed.

(vi) The Chair of the SEC, the Chairman of the CFTC, the Chairman of the Federal Reserve, the Chairperson of the Board of Directors of the Federal Deposit Insurance Corporation, and the Comptroller of the Currency are each encouraged to consider the extent to which investor and market protection measures within their respective jurisdictions may be used to address the risks of digital assets and whether additional measures may be needed.

(vii) Within 180 days of the date of this order, the Director of the Office of Science and Technology Policy, in consultation with the Secretary of the Treasury, the Secretary of Energy, the Administrator of the Environmental Protection Agency, the Chair of the Council of Economic Advisers, the Assistant to the President and National Climate Advisor, and the heads of other relevant agencies, shall submit a report to the President on the connections between distributed ledger technology and short-, medium-, and long-term economic and energy transitions; the potential for these technologies to impede or advance efforts to tackle climate change at home and abroad; and the impacts these technologies have on the environment. This report shall be coordinated through the interagency process described in section 3 of this order. The report should also address the effect of cryptocurrencies' consensus mechanisms on energy usage, including research into potential mitigating measures and alternative mechanisms of consensus and the design tradeoffs those may entail. The report should specifically address:

(A) potential uses of blockchain that could support monitoring or mitigating technologies to climate impacts, such as exchanging of liabilities for greenhouse gas emissions, water, and other natural or environmental assets; and

(B) implications for energy policy, including as it relates to grid management and reliability, energy efficiency incentives and standards, and sources of energy supply.

(viii) Within 1 year of submission of the report described in section 5(b)(vii) of this order, the Director of the Office of Science and Technology Policy, in consultation with the Secretary of the Treasury, the Secretary of Energy, the Administrator of the Environmental Protection Agency, the Chair of the Council of Economic Advisers, and the heads of other relevant agencies, shall update the report described in section 5(b)(vii) of this order, including to address any knowledge gaps identified in such report.

Sec. 6. *Actions to Promote Financial Stability, Mitigate Systemic Risk, and Strengthen Market Integrity.* (a) Financial regulators—including the SEC, the CFTC, and the CFPB and Federal banking agencies—play critical roles in establishing and overseeing protections across the financial system that safeguard its integrity and promote its stability. Since 2017, the Secretary of the Treasury has convened the Financial Stability Oversight Council (FSOC) to assess the financial stability risks and regulatory gaps posed by the ongoing adoption of digital assets.

The United States must assess and take steps to address risks that digital assets pose to financial stability and financial market integrity.

(b) Within 210 days of the date of this order, the Secretary of the Treasury should convene the FSOC and produce a report outlining the specific financial stability risks and regulatory gaps posed by various types of digital assets and providing recommendations to address such risks. As the Secretary of the Treasury and the FSOC deem appropriate, the report should consider the particular features of various types of digital assets and include recommendations that address the identified financial stability risks posed by these digital assets, including any proposals for additional or adjusted regulation and supervision as well as for new legislation. The report should take account of the prior analyses and assessments of the FSOC, agencies, and the President's Working Group on Financial Markets, including the ongoing work of the Federal banking agencies, as appropriate.

Sec. 7. *Actions to Limit Illicit Finance and Associated National Security Risks.* (a) Digital assets have facilitated sophisticated cybercrime-related financial networks and activity, including through ransomware activity.

The growing use of digital assets in financial activity heightens risks of crimes such as money laundering, terrorist and proliferation financing, fraud and theft schemes, and corruption. These illicit activities highlight the need for ongoing scrutiny of the use of digital assets, the extent to which technological innovation may impact such activities, and exploration of opportunities to mitigate these risks through regulation, supervision, public-private engagement, oversight, and law enforcement.

(b) Within 90 days of submission to the Congress of the National Strategy for Combating Terrorist and Other Illicit Financing, the Secretary of the Treasury, the Secretary of State, the Attorney General, the Secretary of Commerce, the Secretary of Homeland Security, the Director of the Office of Management and Budget, the Director of National Intelligence, and the heads of other relevant agencies may each submit to the President supplemental annexes, which may be classified or unclassified, to the Strategy offering additional views on illicit finance risks posed by digital assets, including cryptocurrencies, stablecoins, CBDCs, and trends in the use of digital assets by illicit actors.

(c) Within 120 days of submission to the Congress of the National Strategy for Combating Terrorist and Other Illicit Financing, the Secretary of the Treasury, in consultation with the Secretary of State, the Attorney General, the Secretary of Commerce, the Secretary of Homeland Security, the Director of the Office of Management and Budget, the Director of National Intelligence, and the heads of other relevant agencies shall develop a coordinated action plan based on the Strategy's conclusions for mitigating the digital-asset-related illicit finance and national security risks addressed in the updated strategy. This action plan shall be coordinated through the interagency process described in section 3 of this order. The action plan shall address the role of law enforcement and measures to increase financial services providers' compliance with AML/CFT obligations related to digital asset activities.

(d) Within 120 days following completion of all of the following reports—the National Money Laundering Risk Assessment; the National Terrorist Financing Risk Assessment; the National Proliferation Financing Risk Assessment; and the updated National Strategy for Combating Terrorist and Other Illicit Financing—the Secretary of the Treasury shall notify the relevant agencies through the interagency process described in section 3 of this order on any pending, proposed, or prospective rulemakings to address digital asset illicit finance risks.

The Secretary of the Treasury shall consult with and consider the perspectives of relevant agencies in evaluating opportunities to mitigate such risks through regulation.

Sec. 8. *Policy and Actions Related to Fostering International Cooperation and United States Competitiveness.* (a) The policy of my Administration on fostering international cooperation and United States competitiveness with respect to digital assets and financial innovation is as follows:

(i) Technology-driven financial innovation is frequently cross-border and therefore requires international cooperation among public authorities. This cooperation is critical to maintaining high regulatory standards and a level playing field.

Uneven regulation, supervision, and compliance across jurisdictions creates opportunities for arbitrage and raises risks to financial stability and the protection of consumers, investors, businesses, and markets. Inadequate AML/CFT regulation, supervision, and enforcement by other countries challenges the ability of the United States to investigate illicit digital asset transaction flows that frequently jump overseas, as is often the case in ransomware payments and other cybercrime-related money laundering. There must also be cooperation to reduce inefficiencies in international funds transfer and payment systems.

(ii) The United States Government has been active in international fora and through bilateral partnerships on many of these issues and has a robust agenda to continue this work in the coming years.

While the United States held the position of President of the FATF, the United States led the group in developing and adopting the first international standards on digital assets.

The United States must continue to work with international partners on standards for the development and appropriate interoperability of digital payment architectures and CBDCs to reduce payment inefficiencies and ensure that any new funds transfer and payment systems are consistent with United States values and legal requirements.

(iii) While the United States held the position of President of the 2020 G7, the United States established the G7 Digital Payments Experts Group to discuss CBDCs, stablecoins, and other digital payment issues.

The G7 report outlining a set of policy principles for CBDCs is an important contribution to establishing guidelines for jurisdictions for the exploration and potential development of CBDCs. While a CBDC would be issued by a country's central bank, the supporting infrastructure could involve both public and private participants. The G7 report highlighted that any CBDC should be grounded in the G7's long-standing public commitments to transparency, the rule of law, and sound economic governance, as well as the promotion of competition and innovation.

(iv) The United States continues to support the G20 roadmap for addressing challenges and frictions with cross-border funds transfers and payments for which work is underway, including work on improvements to existing systems for cross-border funds transfers and payments, the international dimensions of CBDC designs, and the potential of well-regulated stablecoin arrangements. The international Financial Stability Board (FSB), together with standard-setting bodies, is leading work on issues related to stablecoins, cross-border funds transfers and payments, and other international dimensions of digital assets and payments, while FATF continues its leadership in setting AML/CFT standards for digital assets. Such international work should continue to address the full spectrum of issues and challenges raised by digital assets, including financial stability, consumer, investor, and business risks, and money laundering, terrorist financing, proliferation financing, sanctions evasion, and other illicit activities.

(v) My Administration will elevate the importance of these topics and expand engagement with our critical international partners, including through fora such as the G7, G20, FATF, and FSB.

My Administration will support the ongoing international work and, where appropriate, push for additional work to drive development and implementation of holistic standards, cooperation and coordination, and information sharing. With respect to digital assets, my Administration will seek to ensure that our core democratic values are respected; consumers, investors, and businesses are protected; appropriate global financial system connectivity and platform and architecture interoperability are preserved; and the safety and soundness of the global financial system and international monetary system are maintained.

(b) In furtherance of the policy stated in section 8(a) of this order:

(i) Within 120 days of the date of this order, the Secretary of the Treasury, in consultation with the Secretary of State, the Secretary of Commerce, the Administrator of the United States Agency for International Development, and the heads of other relevant agencies, shall establish a framework for interagency international engagement with foreign counterparts and in international fora to, as appropriate, adapt, update, and enhance adoption of global principles and standards for how digital assets are used and transacted, and to promote development of digital asset and CBDC technologies consistent with our values and legal requirements.

This framework shall be coordinated through the interagency process described in section 3 of this order. This framework shall include specific and prioritized lines of effort and coordinated messaging; interagency engagement and activities with foreign partners, such as foreign assistance and capacity-building efforts and coordination of global compliance; and whole-of-government efforts to promote international principles, standards, and best practices. This framework should reflect ongoing leadership by the Secretary of the Treasury and financial regulators in relevant international financial standards bodies, and should elevate United States engagement on digital assets issues in technical standards bodies and other international fora to promote development of digital asset and CBDC technologies consistent with our values.

(ii) Within 1 year of the date of the establishment of the framework required by section 8(b)(i) of this order, the Secretary of the Treasury, in consultation with the Secretary of State, the Secretary of Commerce, the Director of the Office of Management and Budget, the Administrator of the United States Agency for International Development, and the heads of other relevant agencies as appropriate, shall submit a report to the President on priority actions taken under the framework and its effectiveness. This report shall be coordinated through the interagency process described in section 3 of this order.

(iii) Within 180 days of the date of this order, the Secretary of Commerce, in consultation with the Secretary of State, the Secretary of the Treasury, and the heads of other relevant agencies, shall establish a framework for enhancing United States economic competitiveness in, and leveraging of, digital asset technologies.

This framework shall be coordinated through the interagency process described in section 3 of this order.

(iv) Within 90 days of the date of this order, the Attorney General, in consultation with the Secretary of State, the Secretary of the Treasury, and the Secretary of Homeland Security, shall submit a report to the President on how to strengthen international law enforcement cooperation for detecting, investigating, and prosecuting criminal activity related to digital assets.

Sec. 9. *Definitions.* For the purposes of this order:

(a) The term "blockchain" refers to distributed ledger technologies where data is shared across a network that creates a digital ledger of verified transactions or information among network participants and the data are typically linked using cryptography to maintain the integrity of the ledger and execute other functions, including transfer of ownership or value.

(b) The term "central bank digital currency" or "CBDC" refers to a form of digital money or monetary value, denominated in the national unit of account, that is a direct liability of the central bank.

(c) The term "cryptocurrencies" refers to a digital asset, which may be a medium of exchange, for which generation or ownership records are supported through a distributed ledger technology that relies on cryptography, such as a blockchain.

(d) The term "digital assets" refers to all CBDCs, regardless of the technology used, and to other representations of value, financial assets and instruments, or claims that are used to make payments or investments, or to transmit or exchange funds or the equivalent thereof, that are issued or represented in digital form through the use of distributed ledger technology. For example, digital assets include cryptocurrencies, stablecoins, and CBDCs. Regardless of the label used, a digital asset may be, among other things, a security, a commodity, a derivative, or other financial product. Digital assets may be exchanged across digital asset trading platforms, including centralized and decentralized finance platforms, or through peer-to-peer technologies.

(e) The term "stablecoins" refers to a category of cryptocurrencies with mechanisms that are aimed at maintaining a stable value, such as by pegging the value of the coin to a specific currency, asset, or pool of assets or by algorithmically controlling supply in response to changes in demand in order to stabilize value.

Sec. 10. *General Provisions.* (a) Nothing in this order shall be construed to impair or otherwise affect:

(i) the authority granted by law to an executive department or agency, or the head thereof; or

(ii) the functions of the Director of the Office of Management and Budget relating to budgetary, administrative, or legislative proposals.

(b) This order shall be implemented consistent with applicable law and subject to the availability of appropriations.

(c) This order is not intended to, and does not, create any right or benefit, substantive or procedural, enforceable at law or in equity by any party against the United States, its departments, agencies, or entities, its officers, employees, or agents, or any other person.

BITCOIN: A PEER TO PEER ELECTRONIC CASH SYSTEM

Satoshi Nakamoto
satoshin@gmx.com
www.bitcoin.org

Abstract. A purely peer-to-peer version of electronic cash would allow online payments to be sent directly from one party to another without going through a financial institution. Digital signatures provide part of the solution, but the main benefits are lost if a trusted third party is still required to prevent double-spending. We propose a solution to the double-spending problem using a peer-to-peer network. The network timestamps transactions by hashing them into an ongoing chain of hash-based proof-of-work, forming a record that cannot be changed without redoing the proof-of-work. The longest chain not only serves as proof of the sequence of events witnessed, but proof that it came from the largest pool of CPU power. As long as a majority of CPU power is controlled by nodes that are not cooperating to attack the network, they'll generate the longest chain and outpace attackers. The network itself requires minimal structure. Messages are broadcast on a best effort basis, and nodes can leave and rejoin the network at will, accepting the longest proof-of-work chain as proof of what happened while they were gone.

1. Introduction

Commerce on the Internet has come to rely almost exclusively on financial institutions serving as trusted third parties to process electronic payments. While the system works well enough for most transactions, it still suffers from the inherent weaknesses of the trust based model. Completely non-reversible transactions are not really possible, since financial institutions cannot avoid mediating disputes. The cost of mediation increases transaction costs, limiting the minimum practical transaction size and cutting off the possibility for small casual transactions, and there is a broader cost in the loss of ability to make non-reversible payments for nonreversible services. With the possibility of reversal, the need for trust spreads. Merchants must be wary of their customers, hassling them for more information than they would otherwise need. A certain percentage of fraud is accepted as unavoidable. These costs and payment uncertainties can be avoided in person by using physical currency, but no mechanism exists to make payments over a communications channel without a trusted party.

What is needed is an electronic payment system based on cryptographic proof instead of trust, allowing any two willing parties to transact directly with each other without the need for a trusted third party. Transactions that are computationally impractical to reverse would protect sellers from fraud, and routine escrow mechanisms could easily be implemented to protect buyers. In this paper, we propose a solution to the double-spending problem using a peer-to-peer distributed timestamp server to generate computational proof of the chronological order of transactions. The system is secure as long as honest nodes collectively control more CPU power than any cooperating group of attacker nodes.

2. Transactions

We define an electronic coin as a chain of digital signatures. Each owner transfers the coin to the next by digitally signing a hash of the previous transaction and the public key of the next owner and adding these to the end of the coin. A payee can verify the signatures to verify the chain of ownership.

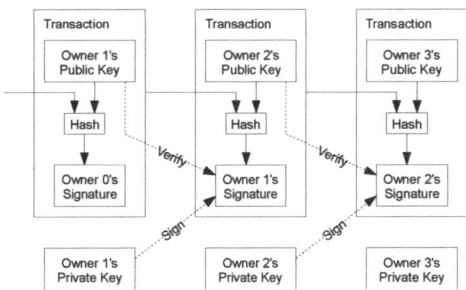

The problem of course is the payee can't verify that one of the owners did not double-spend the coin. A common solution is to introduce a trusted central authority, or mint, that checks every transaction for double spending. After each transaction, the coin must be returned to the mint to issue a new coin, and only coins issued directly from the mint are trusted not to be double-spent. The problem with this solution is that the fate of the entire money system depends on the company running the mint, with every transaction having to go through them, just like a bank. We need a way for the payee to know that the previous owners did not sign any earlier transactions. For our purposes, the earliest transaction is the one that counts, so we don't care about later attempts to double-spend. The only way to confirm the absence of a transaction is to be aware of all transactions. In the mint based model, the mint was aware of all transactions and decided which arrived first. To accomplish this without a trusted party, transactions must be publicly announced [1], and we need a system for participants to agree on a single history of the order in which they were received. The payee needs proof that at the time of each transaction, the majority of nodes agreed it was the first received.

3. Timestamp Server

The solution we propose begins with a timestamp server. A timestamp server works by taking a hash of a block of items to be timestamped and widely publishing the hash, such as in a newspaper or Usenet post [2-5]. The timestamp proves that the data must have existed at the time, obviously, in order to get into the hash. Each timestamp includes the previous timestamp in its hash, forming a chain, with each additional timestamp reinforcing the ones before it.

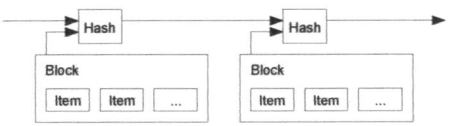

4. Proof-of-Work

To implement a distributed timestamp server on a peer-to-peer basis, we will need to use a proof-of-work system similar to Adam Back's Hashcash [6], rather than newspaper or Usenet posts. The proof-of-work involves scanning for a value that when hashed, such as with SHA-256, the hash begins with a number of zero bits. The average work required is exponential in the number of zero bits required and can be verified by executing a single hash. For our timestamp network, we implement the proof-of-work by incrementing a nonce in the block until a value is found that gives the block's hash the required zero bits. Once the CPU effort has been expended to make it satisfy the proof-of-work, the block cannot be changed without redoing the work. As later blocks are chained after it, the work to change the block would include redoing all the blocks after it.

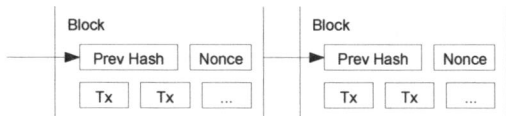

The proof-of-work also solves the problem of determining representation in majority decision making. If the majority were based on one-IP-address-one-vote, it could be subverted by anyone able to allocate many IPs. Proof-of-work is essentially one-CPU-one-vote. The majority decision is represented by the longest chain, which has the greatest proof-of-work effort invested in it. If a majority of CPU power is controlled by honest nodes, the honest chain will grow the fastest and outpace any competing chains. To modify a past block, an attacker would have to redo the proof-of-work of the block and all blocks after it and then catch up with and surpass the work of the honest nodes. We will show later that the probability of a slower attacker catching up diminishes exponentially as subsequent blocks are added. To compensate for increasing hardware speed and varying interest in running nodes over time, the proof-of-work difficulty is determined by a moving average targeting an average number of blocks per hour. If they're generated too fast, the difficulty increases.

5. Network

The steps to run the network are as follows:

1) New transactions are broadcast to all nodes.
2) Each node collects new transactions into a block.
3) Each node works on finding a difficult proof-of-work for its block.
4) When a node finds a proof-of-work, it broadcasts the block to all nodes.
5) Nodes accept the block only if all transactions in it are valid and not already spent.
6) Nodes express their acceptance of the block by working on creating the next block in the chain, using the hash of the accepted block as the previous hash.

Nodes always consider the longest chain to be the correct one and will keep working on extending it. If two nodes broadcast different versions of the next block simultaneously, some nodes may receive one or the other first. In that case, they work on the first one they received, but save the other branch in case it becomes longer. The tie will be broken when the next proofof- work is found and one branch becomes longer; the nodes that were working on the other branch will then switch to the longer one.

6. Incentive

By convention, the first transaction in a block is a special transaction that starts a new coin owned by the creator of the block. This adds an incentive for nodes to support the network, and provides a way to initially distribute coins into circulation, since there is no central authority to issue them. The steady addition of a constant of amount of new coins is analogous to gold miners expending resources to add gold to circulation. In our case, it is CPU time and electricity that is expended.

The incentive can also be funded with transaction fees. If the output value of a transaction is less than its input value, the difference is a transaction fee that is added to the incentive value of the block containing the transaction. Once a predetermined number of coins have entered circulation, the incentive can transition entirely to transaction fees and be completely inflation free. The incentive may help encourage nodes to stay honest. If a greedy attacker is able to assemble more CPU power than all the honest nodes, he would have to choose between using it to defraud people by stealing back his payments, or using it to generate new coins. He ought to find it more profitable to play by the rules, such rules that favour him with more new coins than everyone else combined, than to undermine the system and the validity of his own wealth.

7. Reclaiming Disk Space

Once the latest transaction in a coin is buried under enough blocks, the spent transactions before it can be discarded to save disk space. To facilitate this without breaking the block's hash, transactions are hashed in a Merkle Tree [7][2][5], with only the root included in the block's hash. Old blocks can then be compacted by stubbing off branches of the tree. The interior hashes do not need to be stored.

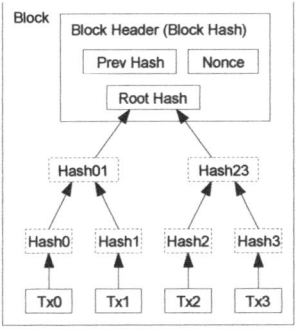

Transactions Hashed in a Merkle Tree

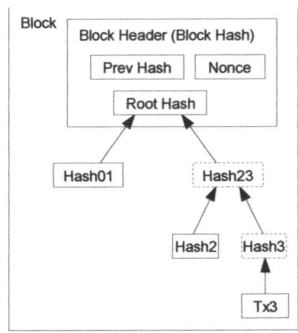

After Pruning Tx0-2 from the Block

A block header with no transactions would be about 80 bytes. If we suppose blocks are generated every 10 minutes, 80 bytes * 6 * 24 * 365 = 4.2MB per year. With computer systems typically selling with 2GB of RAM as of 2008, and Moore's Law predicting current growth of 1.2GB per year, storage should not be a problem even if the block headers must be kept in memory.

8. Simplified Payment Verification

It is possible to verify payments without running a full network node. A user only needs to keep a copy of the block headers of the longest proof-of-work chain, which he can get by querying network nodes until he's convinced he has the longest chain, and obtain the Merkle branch linking the transaction to the block it's timestamped in. He can't check the transaction for himself, but by linking it to a place in the chain, he can see that a network node has accepted it, and blocks added after it further confirm the network has accepted it.

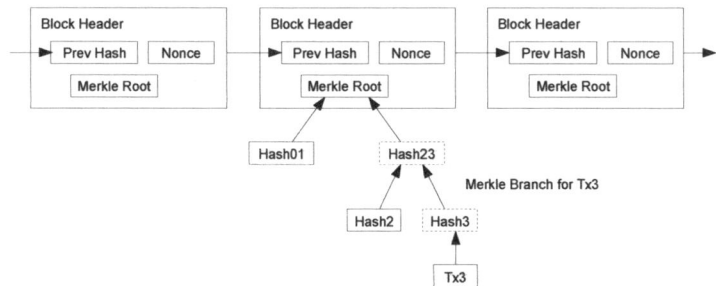

As such, the verification is reliable as long as honest nodes control the network, but is more vulnerable if the network is overpowered by an attacker. While network nodes can verify transactions for themselves, the simplified method can be fooled by an attacker's fabricated transactions for as long as the attacker can continue to overpower the network. One strategy to protect against this would be to accept alerts from network nodes when they detect an invalid block, prompting the user's software to download the full block and alerted transactions to confirm the inconsistency. Businesses that receive frequent payments will probably still want to run their own nodes for more independent security and quicker verification.

9. Combining and Splitting Value

Although it would be possible to handle coins individually, it would be unwieldy to make a separate transaction for every cent in a transfer. To allow value to be split and combined, transactions contain multiple inputs and outputs. Normally there will be either a single input from a larger previous transaction or multiple inputs combining smaller amounts, and at most two outputs: one for the payment, and one returning the change, if any, back to the sender.

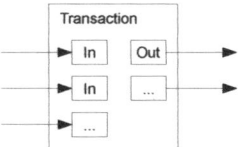

It should be noted that fan-out, where a transaction depends on several transactions, and those transactions depend on many more, is not a problem here. There is never the need to extract a complete standalone copy of a transaction's history.

10. Privacy

The traditional banking model achieves a level of privacy by limiting access to information to the parties involved and the trusted third party. The necessity to announce all transactions publicly precludes this method, but privacy can still be maintained by breaking the flow of information in another place: by keeping public keys anonymous. The public can see that someone is sending an amount to someone else, but without information linking the transaction to anyone. This is similar to the level of information released by stock exchanges, where the time and size of individual trades, the "tape", is made public, but without telling who the parties were.

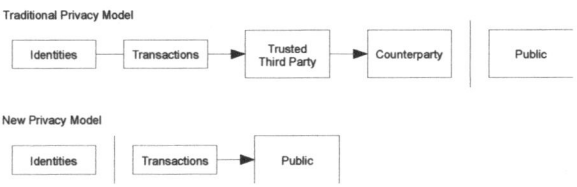

As an additional firewall, a new key pair should be used for each transaction to keep them from being linked to a common owner. Some linking is still unavoidable with multi-input transactions, which necessarily reveal that their inputs were owned by the same owner. The risk is that if the owner of a key is revealed, linking could reveal other transactions that belonged to the same owner.

11. Calculations

We consider the scenario of an attacker trying to generate an alternate chain faster than the honest chain. Even if this is accomplished, it does not throw the system open to arbitrary changes, such as creating value out of thin air or taking money that never belonged to the attacker. Nodes are not going to accept an invalid transaction as payment, and honest nodes will never accept a block containing them. An attacker can only try to change one of his own transactions to take back money he recently spent.

The race between the honest chain and an attacker chain can be characterized as a Binomial Random Walk. The success event is the honest chain being extended by one block, increasing its lead by +1, and the failure event is the attacker's chain being extended by one block, reducing the gap by -1.

The probability of an attacker catching up from a given deficit is analogous to a Gambler's Ruin problem. Suppose a gambler with unlimited credit starts at a deficit and plays potentially an infinite number of trials to try to reach breakeven. We can calculate the probability he ever reaches breakeven, or that an attacker ever catches up with the honest chain, as follows [8]:

p = probability an honest node finds the next block
q = probability the attacker finds the next block
q_z = probability the attacker will ever catch up from z blocks behind

$$q_z = \begin{cases} 1 & \text{if } p \leq q \\ (q/p)^z & \text{if } p > q \end{cases}$$

Given our assumption that p > q, the probability drops exponentially as the number of blocks the attacker has to catch up with increases. With the odds against him, if he doesn't make a lucky lunge forward early on, his chances become vanishingly small as he falls further behind.

We now consider how long the recipient of a new transaction needs to wait before being sufficiently certain the sender can't change the transaction. We assume the sender is an attacker who wants to make the recipient believe he paid him for a while, then switch it to pay back to himself after some time has passed. The receiver will be alerted when that happens, but the sender hopes it will be too late.

The receiver generates a new key pair and gives the public key to the sender shortly before signing. This prevents the sender from preparing a chain of blocks ahead of time by working on it continuously until he is lucky enough to get far enough ahead, then executing the transaction at that moment. Once the transaction is sent, the dishonest sender starts working in secret on a parallel chain containing an alternate version of his transaction.

The recipient waits until the transaction has been added to a block and z blocks have been linked after it. He doesn't know the exact amount of progress the attacker has made, but assuming the honest blocks took the average expected time per block, the attacker's potential progress will be a Poisson distribution with expected value:

$$\lambda = z \frac{q}{p}$$

To get the probability the attacker could still catch up now, we multiply the Poisson density for each amount of progress he could have made by the probability he could catch up from that point:

$$\sum_{k=0}^{\infty} \frac{\lambda^k e^{-\lambda}}{k!} \cdot \begin{cases} (q/p)^{(z-k)} & if\ k \leq z \\ 1 & if\ k > z \end{cases}$$

Rearranging to avoid summing the infinite tail of the distribution...

$$1 - \sum_{k=0}^{z} \frac{\lambda^k e^{-\lambda}}{k!} \left(1 - (q/p)^{(z-k)}\right)$$

Converting to C code...

```
#include <math.h>
double AttackerSuccessProbability(double q, int z)
{
    double p = 1.0 - q;
    double lambda = z * (q / p);
    double sum = 1.0;
    int i, k;
    for (k = 0; k <= z; k++)
    {
        double poisson = exp(-lambda);
        for (i = 1; i <= k; i++)
            poisson *= lambda / i;
        sum -= poisson * (1 - pow(q / p, z - k));
    }
    return sum;
}
```

Running some results, we can see the probability drop off exponentially with z.

```
q=0.1
z=0    P=1.0000000
z=1    P=0.2045873
z=2    P=0.0509779
z=3    P=0.0131722
z=4    P=0.0034552
z=5    P=0.0009137
z=6    P=0.0002428
z=7    P=0.0000647
z=8    P=0.0000173
z=9    P=0.0000046
z=10   P=0.0000012

q=0.3
z=0    P=1.0000000
z=5    P=0.1773523
z=10   P=0.0416605
z=15   P=0.0101008
z=20   P=0.0024804
z=25   P=0.0006132
z=30   P=0.0001522
z=35   P=0.0000379
z=40   P=0.0000095
z=45   P=0.0000024
z=50   P=0.0000006
```

Solving for P less than 0.1%...

```
P < 0.001
q=0.10    z=5
q=0.15    z=8
q=0.20    z=11
q=0.25    z=15
q=0.30    z=24
q=0.35    z=41
q=0.40    z=89
q=0.45    z=340
```

12. Conclusion

We have proposed a system for electronic transactions without relying on trust. We started with the usual framework of coins made from digital signatures, which provides strong control of ownership, but is incomplete without a way to prevent double-spending. To solve this, we proposed a peer-to-peer network using proof-of-work to record a public history of transactions that quickly becomes computationally impractical for an attacker to change if honest nodes control a majority of CPU power. The network is robust in its unstructured simplicity. Nodes work all at once with little coordination. They do not need to be identified, since messages are not routed to any particular place and only need to be delivered on a best effort basis. Nodes can leave and rejoin the network at will, accepting the proof-of-work chain as proof of what happened while they were gone. They vote with their CPU power, expressing their acceptance of valid blocks by working on extending them and rejecting invalid blocks by refusing to work on them. Any needed rules and incentives can be enforced with this consensus mechanism.

BITCOIN: A PEER TO PEER ELECTRONIC CASH SYSTEM - REFERENCES

[1] W. Dai, "b-money," http://www.weidai.com/bmoney.txt, 1998.

[2] H. Massias, X.S. Avila, and J.-J. Quisquater, "Design of a secure timestamping service with minimal trust requirements," In 20th Symposium on Information Theory in the Benelux, May 1999.

[3] S. Haber, W.S. Stornetta, "How to time-stamp a digital document," In Journal of Cryptology, vol 3, no 2, pages 99-111, 1991.

[4] D. Bayer, S. Haber, W.S. Stornetta, "Improving the efficiency and reliability of digital time-stamping," In Sequences II: Methods in Communication, Security and Computer Science, pages 329-334, 1993.

[5] S. Haber, W.S. Stornetta, "Secure names for bit-strings," In Proceedings of the 4th ACM Conference on Computer and Communications Security, pages 28-35, April 1997.

[6] A. Back, "Hashcash - a denial of service counter-measure," http://www.hashcash.org/papers/hashcash.pdf, 2002.

[7] R.C. Merkle, "Protocols for public key cryptosystems," In Proc. 1980 Symposium on Security and Privacy, IEEE Computer Society, pages 122-133, April 1980.

[8] W. Feller, "An introduction to probability theory and its applications," 1957.

ENDNOTES

1. Aro, Robert. "Fedcoin Report Issued." Mises Institute, January 24, 2022. https://mises.org/power-market/fedcoin-report-issued.
2. "Federal Reserve Board Releases Discussion Paper That Examines Pros and Cons of a Potential U.S. Central Bank Digital Currency (CBDC)." Board of Governors of the Federal Reserve System, January 20, 2022. https://www.federalreserve.gov/newsevents/pressreleases/other20220120a.htm.
3. Murphy, Robert P. "It's Not Paranoid to Worry about a Central Bank Digital Currency." Mises Institute, April 17, 2023. https://mises.org/mises-wire/its-not-paranoid-worry-about-central-bank-digital-currency.
4. Biden, Joseph R. "Ensuring Responsible Development of Digital Assets." Federal Register, March 14, 2022. https://www.federalregister.gov/documents/2022/03/14/2022-05471/ensuring-responsible-development-of-digital-assets.
5. "Ensuring Responsible Development of Digital Assets." The Federal Register. The National Archives, March 14, 2022. https://www.federalregister.gov/documents/2022/03/14/2022-05471/ensuring-responsible-development-of-digital-assets.
6. "Boston Fed, MIT Complete Research Project into Feasibility of a Central Bank Digital Currency." Federal Reserve Bank of Boston, December 22, 2022. https://www.bostonfed.org/news-and-events/news/2022/12/project-hamilton-boston-fed-mit-complete-central-bank-digital-currency-cbdc-project.aspx.
7. "First Bank of the United States." Wikimedia Foundation, January 13, 2020. https://en.wikipedia.org/wiki/First_Bank_of_the_United_States.
8. Brands, H. W. (2011). Greenback Planet: How the Dollar Conquered the World and Threatened Civilization as We Know It. University of Texas Press. ISBN 9780292739338.
9. Paul, Ron; Lewis, Lehrman (1982). The Case for Gold: A Minority Report of the U.S. Gold Commission (PDF). Auburn, AL: Cato Institute. p. 79. ISBN 0-932790-31-3.
10. Eichengreen, Barry. "Globalizing Capital: A History of the International Monetary System" (3rd ed.). Princeton University Press. p. 7. doi:10.2307/j.ctvd58rxg.
11. Morrison, James Ashley (2016). "Shocking Intellectual Austerity: The Role of Ideas in the Demise of the Gold Standard in Britain." International Organization. 70 (1): 175–207. doi:10.1017/S0020818315000314.
12. Greenspan, Alan. "Gold and Economic Freedom." Scribd. Accessed September 11, 2024. https://www.scribd.com/document/63307491/GREENSPAN-Gold-and-Economic-Freedom.
13. "Executive Order 6102." Wikimedia Foundation, August 29, 2024. https://en.wikipedia.org/wiki/Executive_Order_6102.
14. "US Inflation Calculator." CoinNews. Accessed August 23, 2024. https://www.usinflationcalculator.com/.
15. "Perry v. United States - 294 U.S. 330 (1935)." Supreme.justia.com. Archived from the original on 2013-05-18. Retrieved 2013-12-30.
16. United States Congress (August 14, 1974). "An Act to provide for increased participation by the United States in the International Development Association and to permit United States citizens to purchase, hold, sell, or otherwise deal with gold in the United States or abroad." Pub. L. 93–373. Archived from the original on May 21, 2013. Retrieved August 14, 2021.
17. Ghizoni, Sandra Kollen. "Creation of the Bretton Woods System." Federal Reserve History, November 22, 2013. https://www.federalreservehistory.org/essays/bretton-woods-created.

ENDNOTES

18. Chen, James. "Bretton Woods Agreement and the Institutions It Created Explained." Investopedia, July 2, 2024. https://www.investopedia.com/terms/b/brettonwoodsagreement.asp#citation-1.
19. "World Debt Clock." US Debt Clock. Accessed August 18, 2024. https://usdebtclock.org/world-debt-clock.html.
20. "Major Foreign Holders of U.S. Treasury Securities 2020." Statista. n.d. https://www.statista.com/statistics/246420/major-foreign-holders-of-us-treasury-debt/.
21. Fox, Michelle. "The U.S. National Debt Is Rising by $1 Trillion about Every 100 Days." CNBC, March 1, 2024. https://www.cnbc.com/2024/03/01/the-us-national-debt-is-rising-by-1-trillion-about-every-100-days.html.
22. Lopez, Oscar, and Ephrat Livni. "In Global First, El Salvador Adopts Bitcoin as Currency." The New York Times, September 7, 2021. https://www.nytimes.com/2021/09/07/world/americas/el-salvador-bitcoin.html.
23. "Working with Visa to Break down Barriers in Cross-Border Payments." Swift, September 19, 2023. https://www.swift.com/news-events/news/working-visa-break-down-barriers-cross-border-payments.
24. "OpenCBDC." MIT Digital Currency Initiative, February 10, 2023. https://dci.mit.edu/opencbdc.
25. Haskins, Justin. "Biden Is Planning a New Digital Currency. Here's Why You Should Be Very Worried." The Hill, March 26, 2022. https://thehill.com/opinion/finance/599768-biden-is-planning-a-new-digital-currency-heres-why-you-should-be-very-worried/.
26. Sung, Michael, and Christopher A. Thomas. "The Innovator's Dilemma and U.S. Adoption of a Digital Dollar." Brookings, March 24, 2022. https://www.brookings.edu/articles/the-innovators-dilemma-and-u-s-adoption-of-a-digital-dollar/.
27. Nakamoto, Satoshi. "Bitcoin: A Peer-To-Peer Electronic Cash System." Bitcoin, 2008. https://bitcoin.org/bitcoin.pdf.
28. "Why Decentralization Matters." Ledger, May 15, 2023. https://www.ledger.com/academy/crypto/why-decentralization-matters.
29. Polumbo, Brad. "Why a 'Digital Dollar' Is a Really Bad Idea." Foundation for Economic Education, September 13, 2022. https://fee.org/articles/why-a-digital-dollar-is-a-really-bad-idea/.
30. Jackson, Reuben. "CBDCs: The Good, the Bad, and the Ugly." Crunchbase News, August 3, 2021. https://news.crunchbase.com/fintech-ecommerce/cbdcs-the-good-the-bad-and-the-ugly/.
31. Allcot, Dawn. "US Dollar Value Is Plummeting—What Does This Mean for You?" Yahoo! Finance, June 30, 2023. https://finance.yahoo.com/news/us-dollar-value-plummeting-does-162347145.html.
32. Mercola, Joseph. "Microchip Implanted in Your Hand? Why Worry?" The Defender. Children's Health Defense, April 21, 2022. https://childrenshealthdefense.org/defender/microchip-implanted-hand-cola/.
33. Canales, Katie, and Aaron Mok. "China's 'Social Credit' System Ranks Citizens and Punishes Them with Throttled Internet Speeds and Flight Bans If the Communist Party Deems Them Untrustworthy." Business Insider, November 28, 2022. https://www.businessinsider.com/china-social-credit-system-punishments-and-rewards-explained-2018-4.
34. Donnelly, Drew. "China Social Credit System Explained—What is it & How Does it Work?" Horizons, February 11, 2024. https://joinhorizons.com/china-social-credit-system-explained/.

ENDNOTES

35 Conrad, Jennifer. "China's Digital Yuan Works Just like Cash—with Added Surveillance." Wired, November 8, 2022. https://www.wired.com/story/chinas-digital-yuan-ecny-works-just-like-cash-surveillance/.
36 Conrad, "China's Digital Yuan Works Just like Cash."
37 Conrad, "China's Digital Yuan Works Just like Cash."
38 Canales and Mok. "China's 'Social Credit' System Ranks Citizens."
39 Rahma, Bary. "Exploring the Risks of CBDCs, Digital US Dollars." BeInCrypto, May 1, 2023. https://beincrypto.com/exploring-risks-cbdcs-digital-us-dollar/.
40 Mericle, David, and Laura Nicolae. "US Daily: A Status Report on Central Bank Digital Currencies around the World." Goldman Sachs, May 3, 2021. https://www.gspublishing.com/content/research/en/reports/2021/05/04/a9c1f636-5ac4-4b86-b5c7-9dc89ec37df2.html.
41 "Digital Euro Package." European Parliament, 2023. https://www.europarl.europa.eu/RegData/etudes/BRIE/2023/751477/EPRS_BRI(2023)751477_EN.pdf.
42 Vovan & Lexus. "Prank with the President of the European Central Bank Christine Lagarde." Rumble. Accessed September 10, 2024. https://rumble.com/v2ddlps-prank-with-the-president-of-the-european-central-bank-christine-lagarde.html.
43 "ECB's Lagarde Gets Pranked, Reveals Digital Euro Will Have 'Limited' Control." Yahoo! Finance, April 7, 2023. https://finance.yahoo.com/news/ecb-lagarde-gets-pranked-reveals-135218145.html.
44 "Public Money: Keeping up with the Times." Dutch National Bank, April 5, 2024. https://www.dnb.nl/en/actueel/general-news/2024/speech-2024/public-money-keeping-up-with-the-times/.
45 Michel, Norbert. "There Is No Good Version of a Central Bank Digital Currency." Forbes, April 23, 2024. https://www.forbes.com/sites/digital-assets/2024/04/23/there-is-no-good-version-of-a-central-bank-digital-currency/.
46 Young, Martin. "IMF Touts Programmable and Controllable CBDC for 'Financial Inclusion.'" BeInCrypto, October 17, 2022. https://beincrypto.com/imf-touts-programmable-controllable-cbdc-financial-inclusion/.
47 "Bank for International Settlements." Wikimedia Foundation. Accessed September 11, 2024. https://en.wikipedia.org/wiki/Bank_for_International_Settlements.
48 "How much is 1 ton of gold worth?" Bullion by Post. Accessed September 22, 2023. https://www.bullionbypost.com/index/gold/how-much-is-one-ton-of-gold-worth/.
49 "About BIS - Overview." Bank for International Settlements. Accessed July 13, 2024. https://www.bis.org/about/index.htm.
50 Gurbacs, Gabor. "The Problem with That Statement Is That No-One Hired Central Banks for a Mandate to Have 'Absolute Control' over Money and Dictate Individual Transactions. It's Not within Their Charter. It's Not Their Job or Anyone's as a Matter of Fact. It's Not What People Want Either." X, July 8, 2021. https://x.com/gaborgurbacs/status/1413119906430791686.
51 Scott, Susan V.; Zachariadis, Markos (2014). The Society for Worldwide Interbank Financial Telecommunication (Swift): cooperative governance for network innovation, standards, and community. New York, NY: Routledge. pp. 1, 35. doi:10.4324/9781315849324. ISBN 978-1-317-90952-1. OCLC 862930816.
52 Farrell, Henry; Newman, Abraham L. (July 2019). "Weaponized Interdependence: How Global Economic Networks Shape State Coercion". International Security. 44 (1): 42–79. doi:10.1162/isec_a_00351. ISSN 0162-2889. S2CID 198952367.
53 Seth, Shobhit. "What Is the SWIFT Banking System?" Investopedia, September 14, 2023. https://www.investopedia.com/articles/personal-finance/050515/how-swift-system-works.asp.

ENDNOTES

54 Kenton, Will. "Group of Ten (G10): Definition, Purpose, and Member Countries." Investopedia. Accessed September 11, 2024. https://www.investopedia.com/terms/g/groupoften.asp.
55 Jones, Marc. "SWIFT Planning Launch of New Central Bank Digital Currency Platform in 12-24 Months." Reuters, March 26, 2024. https://www.reuters.com/business/finance/swift-planning-launch-new-central-bank-digital-currency-platform-12-24-months-2024-03-25/.
56 "SWIFT." Wikimedia Foundation, August 19, 2024. https://en.wikipedia.org/wiki/SWIFT#cite_note-10.
57 "SWIFT." Wikimedia Foundation, August 19, 2024. https://en.wikipedia.org/wiki/SWIFT#cite_note-10.
58 Davidson, Charles. "SWIFT's Role in Global Banking." Atlanta Federal Reserve, March 3, 2022. https://www.atlantafed.org/economy-matters/banking-and-finance/2022/03/03/swift-role-in-global-banking.
59 Cipriani, Marco, Linda S. Goldberg, and Gabriele La Spada. "Financial Sanctions, SWIFT, and the Architecture of the International Payments System." The Federal Reserve Bank of New York, January 2023. https://doi.org/10.2139/ssrn.4336483.
60 Jones, Marc. "SWIFT Planning Launch of New Central Bank Digital Currency Platform in 12-24 Months." Reuters, March 26, 2024. https://www.reuters.com/business/finance/swift-planning-launch-new-central-bank-digital-currency-platform-12-24-months-2024-03-25/.
61 Jones, "SWIFT Planning Launch."
62 Shurk, J. B. "Central Bank Digital Currencies: Funny Money That Will Destroy What Is Left of Private Property, Free Markets, and Personal Liberty." Gatestone Institute, April 12, 2023. https://www.gatestoneinstitute.org/19553/central-bank-digital-currencies.
63 Michel, Norbert, "Central Bank Digital Currencies and Freedom Are Incompatible." CATO Institute, July 18, 2022. https://www.cato.org/commentary/central-bank-digital-currencies-freedom-are-incompatible.
64 Michel, "Central Bank Digital Currencies and Freedom Are Incompatible."
65 "Eswar S. Prasad." Cornell University. Accessed September 11, 2024. http://prasad.dyson.cornell.edu/.
66 Michel, "Central Bank Digital Currencies and Freedom Are Incompatible."
67 Smolenski, Natalie, and Dan Held. "The Dangerous Implications of Central Bank Digital Currencies." Bitcoin Magazine, October 3, 2022. https://bitcoinmagazine.com/legal/the-dangerous-implications-of-cbdcs.
68 Bistoletti, Peter. "With the E-Krona, Sweden Is Attacking the Virtues Bitcoin Is Built to Protect." Bitcoin Magazine, May 11, 2023. https://bitcoinmagazine.com/culture/sweden-cbdc-for-financial-surveillance.
69 "Israel Trials CBDC Blockchain Solution That Enables Privacy." Ledger Insights, June 21, 2022. https://www.ledgerinsights.com/israel-cbdc-blockchain-privacy/.
70 Ikeda, Scott. "Proposed 'Digital Rupee' CBDC from India's Central Bank Raises Privacy Concerns." CPO Magazine, January 3, 2022. https://www.cpomagazine.com/data-privacy/proposed-digital-rupee-cbdc-from-indias-central-bank-raises-privacy-concerns/.
71 Gunlock, Julie. "Goodbye Big Gulps in Mayor Bloomberg's New York, Hello Big Government." Forbes, September 18, 2012. https://www.forbes.com/sites/realspin/2012/09/18/goodbye-big-gulps-in-mayor-bloombergs-new-york-hello-big-government.

ENDNOTES

72 W., Shauna. "New York City Board of Health Weighing a Ban on Large Movie Popcorn." ScreenCrush, June 15, 2012. https://screencrush.com/new-york-city-ban-popcorn.
73 Foust, Michael. "LA Mayor Threatens to Shut Off Electricity and Water to Churches that Meet." Crosswalk, August 14, 2020. https://www.crosswalk.com/headlines/contributors/michael-foust/la-mayor-threatens-to-shut-off-electricity-and-water-to-churches-that-meet.html.
74 Kolinovsky, Sarah, and Trish Turner. "Biden Admin Backs down on Tracking Bank Accounts with over $600 Annual Transactions." ABC News, October 19, 2021. https://abcnews.go.com/Politics/biden-admin-backs-tracking-bank-accounts-600-annual/story?id=80665505/.
75 Kolinovsky and Turner. "Biden Admin Backs Down."
76 "CBDCs: Making Payments Programmable." Giesecke+Devrient, March 9, 2023. https://www.gi-de.com/en/spotlight/currency-technology/cbdcs-making-payments-programmable.
77 Kuvvet, Emre. "Sun Shines on Fed 'Doomsday Book.'" The Wall Street Journal, December 11, 2023. https://www.wsj.com/articles/sun-shines-on-new-york-fed-doomsday-book-foia-central-banking-financial-crisis-13d41d51.
78 Anthony, Nicolas. "Digital Currency and the Fed's 'Doomsday Book.'" The Wall Street Journal, December 14, 2023. https://www.wsj.com/articles/fed-digital-currency-cbdc-federal-reserve-1cfa7d8c.
79 Kaminska, Izabella. "Why CBDCs Will Likely Be ID-Based." Financial Times, May 5, 2021. https://www.ft.com/content/88f47c48-97fe-4df3-854e-0d404a3a5f9a.
80 Federal Reserve Chair News Conference," C-SPAN, May 4, 2022. https://www.c-span.org/video/?519938-1/federal-reserve-chair-news-conference.
81 Krugman, Paul. "What Economists (Including Me) Got Wrong about Globalization," Bloomberg, October 10, 2019. https://www.bloomberg.com/view/articles/2019-10-10/inequality-globalization-and-the-missteps-of-1990s-economics.
82 Hirsh, Michael. "Economists on the Run." Foreign Policy, October 22, 2019. https://foreignpolicy.com/2019/10/22/economists-globalization-trade-paul-krugman-china/.
83 Murphy, Robert P. "It's Not Paranoid to Worry about a Central Bank Digital Currency." Mises Institute, April 17, 2023. https://mises.org/mises-wire/its-not-paranoid-worry-about-central-bank-digital-currency.
84 Michel, Norbert, and Nicholas Anthony. "The Risks of CBDCs Why Central Bank Digital Currencies Shouldn't Be Adopted." Cato Institute, February 22, 2023. https://www.cato.org/visual-feature/risks-of-cbdcs.
85 "ArtI.S8.C5.1 Congress's Coinage Power." United States Congress. Accessed August 26, 2024. https://constitution.congress.gov/browse/essay/artI-S8-C5-1/ALDE_00001066/.
86 "31 U.S. Code § 5103 - Legal Tender." Cornell Law School Legal Information Institute. Accessed September 11, 2024. https://www.law.cornell.edu/uscode/text/31/5103.

ABOUT THE AUTHORS

MATHEW D. STAVER, ESQ.

Mathew D. Staver serves as Senior Pastor, Founder, and Chairman of Liberty Counsel; Founder and Chairman of New Revolution; Founder and Chairman of Covenant Journey and Covenant Journey Travel; Founder and Chancellor of Covenant Journey Academy; Chairman of Liberty Counsel Action and Faith and Liberty; Vice President and Chief Counsel of the National Hispanic Christian Leadership Conference; Trustee of Timothy Plan, a family of mutual funds traded in New York and Tel Aviv; and former Dean and Professor of Law at Liberty University School of Law.

Mat has the highest AV rating for attorneys and is board certified in Appellate Practice by the Florida Bar. He has argued before the U.S. Supreme Court. He has published many scholarly and popular articles, brochures, booklets, and books. He is married to Anita, who is President and General Counsel of Liberty Counsel.

STEPHANIE BOWEN

Stephanie Bowen is a Public Policy Analyst and Copywriter for Liberty Counsel. She has extensive experience providing research and policy analysis on a wide range of subjects to some of the nation's best known political and Christian nonprofit leaders, including domestic policy, economics, and international trade agreements.

Her favorite and most life-changing research and analysis is the one that brought her to dedicate her life to Jesus Christ.

ABOUT LIBERTY COUNSEL

LIBERTY COUNSEL

Founded in 1989 by Mat and Anita Staver, Liberty Counsel is one of America's premier Christian legal ministries strategically working to create legal precedent that lasts for generations.

With offices in Florida, Virginia, and Washington, D.C., Liberty Counsel's legal team of experienced and highly skilled attorneys advance the sanctity of human life, religious freedom, and God's design for family.

We accomplish our mission through litigation, education, and public policy. Liberty Counsel's ministry also includes an association of churches dedicated to the preservation of religious freedom.

Liberty Counsel is a firewall for faith and freedom, dedicated to protecting and advancing our God-given rights. "Liberty Counsel will never stop fighting to advance life and liberty. We were born for this moment in history."

—Mathew D. Staver, Esq., Founder and Chairman

ABOUT NEW REVOLUTION

NEW REVOLUTION

New Revolution provides creative communication and printing services to inspire, educate, and transform lives with transcendent truth. We strive to deliver creative solutions that enable our clients to focus on their core missions, particularly in ministry, while we handle the complexities of communication and production.

Founded in 2010, New Revolution is dedicated to supporting and enhancing educational resources rooted in Judeo-Christian thought and values, history, and cultural engagement. We are your trusted partner in transmitting transformative truth through words and symbols, utilizing the latest technology in print, digital media, and laser.

New Revolution offers a comprehensive range of services, including professional editing, graphic design, page layout, cover design, and promotional support, to ensure that every project meets the highest standards of quality. Our state-of-the-art printing capabilities allow us to produce a wide variety of materials, from direct mail and brochures to books, signs, vehicle graphics, wall murals, laser designs, and much more.

New Revolution is your creative solution to achieve your goals in printing, publishing, and marketing. For more information, visit our website, newrevolution.org, or contact us today at 407-875-2100.